ASH

MINDS ON FIRE

ASH

MINDS ON FIRE

Dave Bowler & Bryan Dray

B🍃XTREE

First published in 1997 by Boxtree, an imprint of Macmillan Publishers
Ltd, 25 Eccleston Place, London, SW1W 9NF and Basingstoke

Associated companies throughout the world

ISBN 0 7522 2349 6

Cover designed by Shoot That Tiger!
Inside text and plate section designed by Nigel Davies

Cover photos – front: Redferns, back *left*: Retna, back *right*: Redferns.

Inside Picture Credits
Capital Pictures: pages 3 *bottom*, 4 *top left*, 6
Redferns: pages 4 *bottom*, 5, 7 *top*
Retna: pages 1, 2, 3 *top*, 4 *top right*, 7 *bottom*, 8

9 8 7 6 5 4 3 2 1

A CIP catalogue record for this book is available
from the British Library

Typeset by SX Composing DTP, Rayleigh, Essex
Printed by Mackays of Chatham plc, Chatham, Kent

CONTENTS

DEDICATION

To Mom and Dad
Without whom it would be pointless.
And for Denise
Without whom it would be worthless.
Always

David

To Trish, Emma and Rebecca
For all the love and support.
And Mum, Dad, Joyce and Wal
For their help and patience.

Bryan

ACKNOWLEDGEMENTS

There are a number of people without whom this book would not have been possible and so we would like to pass on our thanks to the following:

Tanja Howarth and Mark Hayward who provide a steady stream of advice and support at very reasonable rates.

Everyone at Boxtree, most notably Emma Mann and Clare Hulton.

Denise Deam who spent far too much of her valuable time helping with all the background work that goes into a book such as this.

Carrie for lots of encouragement – keep reading.

The many and varied inhabitants of cyberspace who helped out via the internet.

The staff of the National Sound Archive and the British Newspaper Library at Colindale who assisted us in our research.

The assorted newspapers and magazines, especially the

legendary *Hot Press*, who provided an invaluable alternative insight into Ash and their music – they are listed as sources at the back of the book.

Mark Wilson at the *Belfast Telegraph*.

The Beatles for the *Anthology* series. How about another dozen videos and CDs from the vaults?

The Conservative Party for providing such entertainment on 1 and 2 May 1997.

And everyone who put their hand in their pockets and forked out for the book. Hope you enjoy it.

INTRODUCTION

It is in the very nature of pop stardom that a band can emerge from apparently nowhere, be around for just a few short months, knock out a handful of singles and yet somehow seem as if they've been the centre of attention forever. The ubiquitous Spice Girls are evidence of that particular phenomenon, but on a more serious musical level other examples can be found. Beatlemania arrived in 1963 and by the end of the year pop's chronologists were hard put to remember the shape of the world before John, Paul, George and Ringo had put their imprint on it. More recently The Stone Roses turned rock music upside down with their unique fusion of traditional indie guitar jangling with a dance floor sensibility which by 1990 dominated everything.

It would be exaggerating things to suggest that Ash have had the same kind of creative impact as either of those two bands, for their musical output to date has been quite conservative, firmly rooted in the traditions of those who have come before. Even so, the hold they have on their audience is a dramatic one. Ash fans are fiercely loyal, devoted to the cause championed by Tim Wheeler, Mark Hamilton and Rick McMurray. Why should Ash be so blessed? Why are their followers so evangelistic in their support? Why did this not happen to Dodgy or Menswear or Gene or any of a clutch of bands that have emerged in the last few years? Ash's secret is a simple one, one that cannot be manufactured. Like The Beatles and The Stone Roses, even The Sex Pistols before them, Ash are their audience. Only more so.

The 'guaranteed real teenagers' angle has been overplayed. Beyond the music press, the wider media has hijacked the Ash bandwagon not because of their musical quality but simply because of their youth. Early headlines professed an amazement that such 'young people' could actually get out of bed in the morning. As the band's success grew, the attitude changed to the corrupting nature of the rock business on these 'young innocents'. Patronising beyond belief, in the aftermath of Ash's rise to glory, the tabloid press could not make up its mind whether all teenagers were bone-idle layabouts who should be put in the army to learn some much needed self-discipline or babes in the wood who needed protecting. Overlooking the fact that by the time 1977 had been unleashed in 1996 the members of Ash were old enough to sample all the delights of the adult world, few could see the music for the artificially stoked outrage. As far as the tabloids were concerned, Ash were not remarkable for their ability but for the fact that had made a record at all at their tender years. The greatest surprise was the failure of the *Sun* to run a 'Twenty Things You Didn't Know About Teenagers' feature, with number one being that 'teenagers are young people aged between thirteen and nineteen'. Such was the level of debate.

Ash's precocity has done them few favours except in the curiosity value they enjoyed early on. But they are not the only people ever to be making great music at an early age. Let us remember that The Beatles were slung out of Hamburg because George Harrison was too young to qualify for a work permit, or that their first appearance on BBC radio came in a show called *Teenager's Turn*. On the release of U2's 'Boy', Larry Mullen had just enjoyed his nineteenth birthday. If we wish to delve back into the musical history books, it can be seen that by the standards set by Mozart, Ash are virtually pensioners. Age is no barrier to the production of worthwhile music or art of any kind. Imagination, or lack of it, provides the only limitations.

That is not to say that their collective youth is not an important part of the story. It is. It has been a vital component of their early success because it ties them to their audience, crucial in gaining the initial attention in which their superbly crafted music could thrive. They have all the same cultural memories as their fans. They have seen the same films, read the same books, bought the same records. They have experienced the same government, lived through the same social upheavals, been equally affected by the death of Kurt Cobain and the advent of the football Premiership. They are at a similar stage of emotional and physical development as most of their army of supporters. They have seen the last twenty years through the same eyes and can empathise with the crowds that come to see them. Equally, their observations about life, the universe and everything strike a chord with that audience that the big bands like R.E.M., U2 or The Cure no longer can since they are separated by a gulf of at least fifteen years and pots of money. Those older bands do not and cannot speak as directly to the new generation of record buyers as Ash can since they are so far removed from their experience.

Reflecting on the Republic of Ireland's greatest rock export, U2, Tim Wheeler sent a chill through an entire generation of ageing rock fans when he noted, 'I remember *The Joshua Tree* coming out and all of that, but really they were sorta before my time.' With such a comment, Wheeler exposed the gulf that exists between artists who emerged in the late 1970s and themselves. Those bands may still make records that are enjoyed by Ash's supporters but they cannot resonate within that audience in the same way that a song like 'Goldfinger' or 'Angel Interceptor' might. Equally, while older fans can find much in Ash's music that is worthy of support, they do not appreciate the adrenaline-fuelled pop in the same way that their contemporaries do – they can understand it, but they cannot feel it. Put more bluntly, Wheeler's view is, 'We deserve to be taken seriously. People just think we're this wacky wee band, a happy bouncy-castle Nirvana. The older people don't fucking get it.'

In that sense – and it is a dangerous position to be in – Ash are genuine spokesmen for their generation. They are not obviously revolutionary in the way that The Sex Pistols were, but by virtue of the fact they had a record deal and were internationally successful as teenagers, their achievement is a laudable, if insidious one and perhaps more important for that. Of all the bands in the world at the moment, they were the ones who refused to accept the conventional wisdom that teenagers do not produce worthwhile artistic statements, that they are incapable of feeling anything, of creating anything, of having a single thought worth expressing. Ash reject the conventional wisdom that anything produced by a sixteen-, seventeen- or eighteen-year-old will be hormonally challenged rubbish, the cloying response to the onset of post-pubescent emotions that cannot be handled. They have proved that to be nonsense and have made it perfectly plain that talent will out whatever the circumstances – if their material lacked depth, if they were a five-minute wonder sold on the strength of their youth, they would have already whacked out three full albums by now. In short, they would be Boyzone, not Ash. And as Tim points out when discussing his compatriots from the south of his island, 'It's not proper music, is it?'

If their relative youth and grasp of the cultural zeitgeist endears them to their peers, their age does have one real drawback. Ash have suffered from the 'too much too young' syndrome. Suddenly finding yourself equipped with wagonloads of money is an enticing prospect for those of us unlikely to realise the dream. Yet if great wads of cash suddenly descend upon you, it can turn into a nightmare. By and large, this is usually via lottery or pools winnings, and generally happens to older people who have their own homes and families and should, if experience of life counts for anything at all, have their heads screwed on. Yet the list of overnight millionaires who have lost the plot is an extensive one. Immense wealth can offer as many problems as it does solutions. If you happen to be fresh out of school when you come into the cash, temptation can be hard to resist. We have seen plenty of footballers go off the rails in similar situations over the years, both at the very top of the game and lower down the scale. Yet a footballer is relatively privileged. His whole life is run for him by his employers, the football club. They oversee his diet, make sure he is in the prime of health, organise his travelling schedules. In addition, he spends his life in one place, able to go home every day after training or a game. In comparison, a musician's life is a kinetic one.

Any rock band that is hitting the road is offered as much free booze as they can quaff, either by the venue or by their fans. The music industry is famed for its seamier side too, with good reason. There is rarely a shortage of hangers on willing to ply wealthy young men with an assortment of pharmaceuticals and such is the schedule foisted on bands that they often succumb to artificial stimulants just to keep going. If they have an interest in recreational drugs or in alcohol, then they are not dissimilar to many of their fans.

But where those simply attending the gig might only have the money to go out and get drunk once a week, for a successful rock band, every night is party night. They have the money to do whatever they like, whenever they like and are under a great deal of pressure to live up to the lifestyle pioneered by their predecessors. It takes huge discipline to turn down all the sensual delights that fame and fortune offer. Rock bands are not renowned for their self-discipline, and especially so those who are off the leash for the very first time.

It is this aspect of Ash life that has caught the attention of the tabloids. While most of the tales have become exaggerated in the telling, there is at least a grain of truth in most of them. And few bands have been as assiduous in embracing riotous living as Ash have over the last couple of years. There is evidence that they have grown weary of the madness and now enjoy the odd bout of relaxation rather than tearing up hotel rooms night after night as though it were a chore. For the sake of their longevity, it is to be hoped that they have moderated their behaviour, for even if only half the tales were true, Ash were on the road to self-destruction. While that would be a personal tragedy for them, it would be a musical tragedy for the rest of us for on the evidence of 1977, they have the potential to become one of the finest bands we have seen in a long, long time. Their songwriting, while not always fully convincing, offers ample hope for a bright future.

Ah yes, the songs. That is what brought Ash to the fore in the first place. The next batch of new material, that which makes up their second paper album, will be crucial to their future. These songs will either consign them to the bargain bins or, more likely, confirm that Ash are indeed a remarkable band. Much is riding on them in this country and abroad. Whether they can withstand that pressure in the future will be a fascinating story, perhaps glorious, perhaps gruesome. They have scarcely emerged unscathed from the first chapters of their story. Yet the trials and tribulations may have made them stronger. If the emotional turmoil feeds into the music, as surely it must, then their second album promises to be a classic. The following pages catalogue the raw material with which they will work.

1.

SELF-BELIEF AND A COUPLE OF GUITARS. AND A GEEK

So it all began in 1977. A little unfair on Rick McMurray perhaps given that he had first seen the light of day in 1975, but then whoever said life was fair? Ash's subsequent glorification of that year has bestowed a certain degree of kudos upon it in the minds of those who scarcely remember it, kudos that is hardly deserved. 1977 was not a vintage year. The country was swamped with union jack merchandise as the Queen celebrated her Silver Jubilee. Punk fashion moved into the high streets too, torn T-shirts inverting the message of patriotism, while a deepening world recession lengthened the dole queues. On the streets of Belfast, bombs and bullets continued to be traded with a tragic regularity. On a lighter note, the year's favourite TV shows were *Charlie's Angels – Baywatch* without the slow motion – and *Starsky and Hutch*. On the sports field, England, Wales and Northern Ireland failed to qualify for the World Cup in Argentina, although Britain did actually manage a Wimbledon Champion – Virginia Wade – and Ian Botham played his first Test match, so not all was doom and gloom. At the movies, the Oscar for best picture went to Woody Allen's *Annie Hall*, though a science-fiction blockbuster, *Star Wars*, picked up six, including one for best original score.

Musically, there were conflicting messages. The number one singles in that year fell to the likes of Johnny Mathis, Donna Summer, Hot Chocolate and Manhattan Transfer, and we were also on the brink of the disco years which followed in the wake of *Saturday Night Fever*. In the album charts, the rock dinosaurs such as Pink Floyd, Bowie and Queen still held sway. That reflected the diversity in tastes that had persisted since The Beatles had hung up their guitars in 1970. Singles were for those with a sweet tooth, while the serious music fans clung to their albums, interrogating the grooves, looking for some sort of spiritual enlightenment amid the endless stream of concept albums turned out by the likes of Gentle Giant, Emerson, Lake & Palmer and Yes. It was a year heavy with musical symbolism too. The first era of rock'n'roll came to an end with the death of its king, Elvis Presley, in August. As his life came to its close, rock music got a much needed shot in the arm as punk made its presence felt, The Sex Pistols' 'God Save The Queen' just missing out on the number one slot in that royal year.

With the selective application of hindsight, 1977 is now seen as some sort of Year One so far as modern music is concerned. Popular legend has it that the New Wave storm-troopers came flying over the barricades, torching everything that had gone before. The truth was more prosaic. Although The Sex Pistols, Siouxsie and the Banshees and

The Clash might have won headlines for their behaviour, they did little to really change the musical status quo, simply adding another genre to the pot. Punk was not the rebirth of popular music, but rather a blood transfusion for an ailing patient. The advent of punk was challenging, reminding everyone that instrumental proficiency was not everything, that having something worthwhile to say was every bit as important as the way that you said it. Ironically, within ten years that manifest truth had been buried once again as pop became increasingly banal and rock increasingly complex. It took Nirvana and the sound of Seattle to clean the slate once more.

Had it not been for Kurt Cobain, Chris Novoselic and Dave Grohl, there might not have been a band called Ash. Or at least, not one worth considering, for it was the release of their seminal *Nevermind* album that galvanised Tim Wheeler and Mark Hamilton into action. Who would have imagined that to be the case when examining their earliest musical interests? The first album that Mark received for Christmas was a Care Bears album. 'They had this Blur/Oasis thing going with The Muppets, who I got the following year. My dad had already told me there was no Santa 'cos he thought it would stop me asking for expensive presents. He was wrong,' said Mark. The first record he actually bought for himself a few years later was an Iron Maiden album, a progression of sorts and one which showed a degree of solidarity with Rick's tastes, his first purchase being an AC/DC single, the title of which has long since been forgotten. Tim's first foray into the record shops was yet more disturbing – 'I bought "Star Trekkin'" by The Firm, which is really rather embarrassing.' Ain't that the truth?

Mark and Tim were born within three months of one another at the start of 1977. Tim made his entrance first, on 4 January. He was born in the small Northern Irish town of Downpatrick, County Down, twenty-five miles south-east of Belfast, just inland from St John's Point. Contrary to popular belief, bombs are not constantly going off all day, every day all over Northern Ireland and consequently places like Downpatrick are not that dissimilar from small provincial towns on the mainland. In that sense, Tim comes from the classic suburban roots of countless rock bands. Divorced from the big city lights and that ephemeral excitement, Downpatrick has its own personality, not the force-fed, carefully cloned attractions of capital city wannabes. Tim explained, 'Downpatrick is much more rock'n'roll than any big city. People are really bored and they go around doing mad things!' Tim grew up in a conventional middle-class environment, causing him to remark later, 'It's fair to say that we're all from stable backgrounds and no one here's going to get into heroin or anything like that.' The normality of his upbringing is underlined by the fact that his mother was a teacher, his father a magistrate and so something of a legal expert who was later to run his eye over the music business contracts that his son would have to sign.

Mark and Tim teamed up in the course of their studies

at Down High School. Mark might well have been one of the people going round 'doing mad things' that Tim had mentioned. Born on 21 March 1977, Mark soon had a very highly developed sense of getting himself into trouble: 'When I was young and at the child minder's house, I was on this wee tricycle and I was an Evel Knievel fan. I came flying down the staircase and through a glass door. I had to get loads of stitches in my head. That was good'. Such off-hand descriptions of accidents and escapades come easily to Mark, so much so that he reminds you of no-one more than Adrian Edmondson's portrayal of Vyvyan in *The Young Ones*, though *Hot Press* likened him to Father Jack from *Father Ted* because of his drinking habits, when perhaps really he is closer to the hapless Dougal. (Rick would of course be Mrs Doyle.) Every time Mark launches into another one of his seemingly endless supply of stories of injury and innocent stupidity, you can only wonder why his life has not already been turned into a situation comedy. Still, there is plenty of time yet.

At school, Mark was a natural when it came to landing himself in trouble. His alleged fondness for acts of petty mindless vandalism, of which more later, suggest that had he not found a guitar in his Christmas stocking in 1989, the adult world might have been a pretty harrowing experience for him. Despite a lack of any malice in his actions, his enquiring mind and rampant curiosity in wanting to experience first-hand the consequences of letting off a fire extinguisher, for example, is not the kind of behaviour that endears itself to the wider world unless you have the excuse of being in a rock'n'roll band and living out the expected lifestyle. Certainly not a vindictive sort, Mark is an innocent abroad, whose full-on enjoyment of life can simply be too much for the authorities. Mark is the man who managed to land himself in trouble with the Nottingham chapter of the Hell's Angels, never the wisest of career moves. From his point of view, it was another harmless prank, an enjoyable part of the life of a rock star: 'All that happened was I squirted this guy with my water pistol. I thought it was funny, he was sober and didn't, and now him and his biker mates want to break my legs.' An intellectual butterfly who is always looking to move on to the next thing, Tim has described Mark as having 'the attention span of a small soap dish'.

As one who does enjoy life to the full, music held obvious attractions for Mark. Recovering from his early brush with the Care Bears, he embraced heavy metal with his customary zeal. The late 1980s were a hugely successful time for the hard rock bands like Aerosmith, Metallica, Bon Jovi, Def Leppard and Iron Maiden, all acts who sold enormous quantities of records with negligible support from the mainstream music press. Just as their image prescribes, these metal bands were the outsiders of the musical fraternity, playing up to the 'nobody loves us but we don't care' ideal that is so appealing to like-minded individuals around the globe. With Mark already hating the idea of school and the thought of a normal life, passing through college or university and on into a dead end job, the apparently wild, cowboy-like rock'n'roll world was a thrilling escape. Not only was he a fan but so was Tim, who admitted to rifling through his elder brother's collection of 'bad heavy metal records'. The two twelve-year-olds were smitten by the idea of leather jackets, loud guitars, loose women and lots of free drink, and they made their first pilgrimage to a live gig together in January 1990, to see Bon Jovi at the King's Hall in Belfast. The experience was a pivotal one for them, fundamental in firing their enthusiasm for forming their own band and getting out of Downpatrick to see the world. Mark was already set on living the life of the inveterate rock'n'roller, admitting, 'There's a pub in Downpatrick that'll serve anyone who's got money, so when I was thirteen I went in there, drank a dozen pints and fell down the stairs in front of my mom when I got home.' While he might be exaggerating about the exact amount he had knocked back, the gist of the story seems true enough, an early example of his love of the high life that was to bring its own complications in due course.

Armed with their shiny new guitars, both Tim and Mark set to work mastering their instruments over the course of the next year or so, fondly dreaming that the day would come when they would become the next Rock Gods, that they would have amps that turned up to eleven and that they would headline the Donnington festival in front of the dandruff ridden thousands. By 1991, they were determined to move on from such idle daydreaming and put their ideas to a more practical use. The long trek towards international stardom began with a single step. Sadly, it was in the wrong direction.

Along with about a dozen class mates, Mark and Tim had been fantasising about starting a band of their own. When push finally came to shove though, most of them dropped out of the running, but there were enough enthusiasts left to form a group. Tim played guitar, Mark bass and they were joined by Malcolm King on rhythm guitar, Andy McLean on drums and singer Gareth 'Cookie' Hutchinson. Like all good putative metal bands, their name needed to conjure up powerful visions of death, destruction and similar good times for all. They chose the moniker Vietnam, which is pretty ironic when you consider that the Vietnam war had ended long before their birth and that they were a band from Northern Ireland where a civil war had been raging for far longer than that in south-east Asia, though thankfully the Irish troubles were generally less bloody and dramatic, nor characterised by the use of napalm or saturation bombing.

Tim's recollections of the time are vivid and he is perfectly happy to embarrass himself with the memories. 'In Vietnam, it was all original stuff, mainly because we weren't good enough to work out any covers. Our heroes were Iron Maiden and David Lee Roth. Everyone else was into The Cure or Morrissey at the time but we were playing these songs about hard loving women in the heart of the city. We'd go on a 1991 World Tour of Friends' Parties and pretend that the garage or bedroom was Madison Square Gardens. We were wearing studded wrist watches and Megadeth T-shirts. It was sad! The vibe we had at the time was the more complicated, the better.' There are still aspects of those roots to be heard in the later Ash material, for a lot of *1977* is influenced as much by Thin Lizzy as it is by the likes of The Buzzcocks, and a good thing too for such diversity is an important part of their appeal. For evidence of that, we need only look at the way Ash have been fêted by magazines as diverse as *Smash Hits* and *Kerrang!*

It is also important to remember that while heavy metal gets a pretty bad press, plenty of good music has come out of the genre and there are some excellent songwriters operating there. For every dismal comedy act like W.A.S.P., you can cite a band like Thin Lizzy or Aerosmith, or even Led Zeppelin, who are too often dismissed as a mere metal band. In spite of the cool-damaging connotations, Tim still defends heavy metal as a viable and important form of music. 'There is no way you can say that all heavy metal is crap because it isn't. We were up our own arses at the time but beneath the screaming guitars and wailing vocals there was always some sort of melody.'

Oddly for a band that has glorified its very youth so much in recent years, Vietnam were rather self-conscious about their tender years. That explained the presence of Andy McLean as their drummer, Tim pointing out, 'He was eighteen and he seemed really old to the rest of us [who were fourteen] – he was a *man*!' Despite these credentials, McLean was, according to Tim, 'the worst drummer ever, so he fitted in well with us'. If McLean was no virtuoso, then Gareth Hutchinson was little better. Tim's assessment was a simple one. 'We had a singer who couldn't sing.'

Given these rather obvious drawbacks and the fact that Tim and Mark made it pretty clear that they were unimpressed with the direction in which things were heading, it comes as no surprise to learn that pretty soon after Vietnam's launch 'we were the laughing stock of Downpatrick – it was bad news'. Hutchinson and McLean quickly got fed up with the group and stopped attending the regular practice sessions that provided a break from the school routine and to which Tim and Mark were utterly committed. That kind of attitude meant that Vietnam would never improve, never pick up fans or gain respect in their locale. A parting of the ways sooner or later was inevitable and early on in 1992, Vietnam came to a grinding halt. Tim recalls, 'We just sort of fell out with the other guys in the band.'

With the exception of the fashion world – itself an adjunct of the rock business – there is nothing so ephemeral, so fast and furious and so constantly in a state of flux as the popular music industry. To term it volatile is to err on the side of caution, for in pop music there are few certainties. When Mark and Tim first caught the musical bug back in 1989, the big bands came from the metal fraternity. Iron Maiden claimed a number one single the year before, Bon Jovi were selling records like it was going out of fashion and so it was unsurprising that they should provide the music of choice for the two youngsters. Metal always had an appeal to the young, partly because of its cartoon-like imagery, but it suffered from a lack of exposure. When, as at the end of the 1980s, it was being served up regularly on TV and radio, it was bound to make inroads into the musical mainstream.

If you had metal on the one hand, then on the other there was the ultra-bland sounds of Mariah Carey or Whitney Houston, or the continuing saga of Michael Jackson while in the 'alternative' rock sphere, U2 had lain low since 1988's *Rattle And Hum*, R.E.M. taking up the mantle of 'world's greatest rock'n'roll band' with the release of *Green* and then *Out Of Time* early in 1991. Little new was coming to the fore to break the cosy arrangement that these three forms of music had at the top of the charts, with rap still comparatively marginalised, at least in the UK. As musical roles started to solidify, it was obvious that a breath of fresh air was needed, a new form capable of shaking the tree.

That sound came from the unlikely city of Seattle in north-west America. The grunge sound was quickly commodified and neutralised but back in 1991 when Nirvana unleashed their epochal *Nevermind* album, they were a bolt from the blue, a wake-up call to all those who were happily accepting the sub-standard fare that was on offer elsewhere. Nirvana offered a new sound and, more important, a new attitude, an attitude that had not been seen in fifteen years since the arrival of punk. It is impossible to under-estimate the impact that Nirvana and those, such as Pearl Jam, who followed in their wake had on the music scene. In one fell swoop, they legitimised what had been the underground sound of independently minded acts, proving to the record companies that their music was commercially viable and might even usurp the more familiar rock acts who were then central to their financial planning.

The emergence of Nirvana could not have been more timely for the future of rock'n'roll. Their powerful energy caught the attention of their audience in the same way that heavy metal did and yet the music was created with a wholly different sensibility. Gone were the spandex trousers, the often gormless lyrics, the gory sub-horror movie connotations and the huge, unwieldy light shows. In its place, Nirvana were offering a new stripped down version of metal with all the musical clout in terms of volume but adding greater musical intelligence to the mix, a sense of melody that if unusual, had its genesis in the classic pop songwriting of The Beatles and the Stones.

Kurt Cobain's songs had a bristling intelligence about them, making no concessions to the dictates of fashion but steadfastly going their own way. Although grunge fashion quickly made it to the centre of the catwalk, the sound of Seattle had nothing to do with such trivialities. It was music that came straight from the heart and connected with an ever expanding audience tired of songs of sorcery or devil worship or hard loving men. Nirvana were human, vulnerable, tuneful and powerful. Their attack on the apathy of Generation X was timely and honest, a necessary kick in the pants for their peers. In short, they were the perfect mix for their time.

As far as Tim and Mark were concerned, they had received some forewarning of just how Nirvana would sound and how popular they might be. At the very time that Vietnam were being laughed off stage in Downpatrick, a group of contemporaries under the promising moniker of Laser Gun Nun were winning the praise they themselves sought. Laser Gun Nun, later to evolve into Backwater, were blasting out their readings of songs by Iggy and the Stooges, a band that were perhaps the Godfathers of the original punk movement, and one to whom Nirvana clearly owed a debt too. The more they saw and heard Laser Gun Nun who played, according to Tim 'at 100 miles an hour', the more excited and the more convinced Mark and Tim became that this was the sound they should adopt. Nirvana's arrival merely confirmed their suspicions that music could be much more than the confines of metal suggested.

Once 'Smells Like Teen Spirit' had made its presence felt in the international market place, things would never be the same again for heavy metal. Nirvana had shown just how redundant metal had become, how it disappeared into a cul-de-sac of its own creation, how it no longer had real resonance or relevance. Back in Downpatrick, Tim and Mark were picking up on the messages coming from across the Atlantic, messages which spelled doom for Vietnam. Never again would they commit themselves solely to the heavy metal sound.

The lackadaisical attitude of Andy McLean and Gareth Hutchinson towards Vietnam was not the only reason for the band falling apart early in 1992. Tim and Mark were undergoing a radical shift in their musical tastes and were looking into the possibility of producing a different kind of sound together. The importance of Nirvana to their future direction cannot be understated – as late as 1996, Mark was informing the press that he bought two copies of any magazines that featured Nirvana so that he might keep one in pristine condition, while cutting the other up to cover his walls at home: 'You need to see my room to believe it,' he confirmed, 'it's a shrine to Nirvana. There is not a square inch of my walls that aren't covered.' However, even had Kurt and company not arrived on the scene, it is probable that Tim and Mark would have moved away from the sound of thundering drums and twiddly guitars. No mere metal heads, they were followers of great pop music too. Mark explained, 'We get the pop sound from stuff like Abba. Mine and Tim's mum are big Abba fans.' Tim had also stumbled upon Paul McCartney's facility for bashing out a great pop standard: 'One of the first records I really fell in love with was *Venus And Mars* by Wings. When my big brother moved out of the house, all he left me with was a tape recorder and a cassette of that.' As well as going a long way towards explaining Tim's bent for great pop songwriting, the love of that record suggests another reason, beyond their collective obsession with *Star Wars*, for the outer space imagery that Ash often use.

Tim's prosaic comment on their changing tastes is 'we started getting into decent music when we were fifteen', but there was more to their determination to forge ahead with their musical project than a matter of taste. Having started Vietnam just for something to do to break up the monotony of everyday life in a small town, their aims were starting to change, their horizons broaden. With exams and career decisions looming ever closer by the day, Tim realised he wanted a new direction.

'I wanted to be a rock star. We always said we wanted something more from life. The typical thing was to work hard at school, go to university and get a job. But life shouldn't be about that. It's about being loved and fucking adored and all that stuff. It was about not being conventional, not fitting in with society, being free. we just wanted to feel more significant than just doing a job and dying. The glamorous lifestyle of rock'n'roll appealed to us.'

These are not unusual dreams. Find any group of fifteen-year-olds and the vast bulk of them would love to trade in the workaday world for a life filled with money and excitement, but then reality bites and the majority settle down to making the best of what is on offer. The difference between most of us and the likes of Tim Wheeler is that he never thought of giving up on the dreams he had. As he pointed out later, 'Self-belief, that is all you need. Self-belief and a couple of guitars,' which as a philosophy sounds rather more plausible than Bono's tongue-in-cheek observation that what you really need is 'three chords and the truth'.

To have the requisite level of self-belief, you also need a great ego, an inner voice that drives you on because you know you've got something worthwhile to offer, something that the rest of the world will pay good money for. Given that Vietnam had been so mind-numbingly dismal, and that time was fairly galloping along, now was the time for Tim and Mark to find out whether they had the songwriting ability to go with their drive to succeed. Following Vietnam's demise, the two spent the next few weeks in time honoured, Lennon and McCartney fashion, holed up in Tim's bedroom after school, practising the songwriting art, Tim taking the lead as Mark came to terms with the bass guitar – one story suggests that he had to learn with three rather than four strings because he couldn't afford the fourth, but there seems to be little truth in that. Tim's memory is that 'we picked things up pretty quickly between us', and certainly they started to amass a catalogue of material. They also had a goal. Tim made it clear that 'we wanted to form a punk band'.

As school finished for the summer break in 1992, Tim and Mark were the proud owners of a clutch of original material which they were longing to play. The next problem they faced was in finding a drummer they could rely on. Their less than impressive track record as Vietnam meant they were hardly in a position to trade on their musical past when trying to find their missing link. Downpatrick's collective memory of the young metal masters was a pretty hostile one, treating them as a joke. One such cynic was Rick McMurray, eighteen months older than both Mark and Tim and already an A-level student. Born in Larne, County Antrim on 11 July 1975, McMurray had enjoyed a similar upbringing to that of his future colleagues. With a bank manager for a father, Rick was also from a secure, middle-class family and had shared their early passion for hard rock staples, his first gig being Aerosmith in Belfast, in November 1989, having been musically educated by his brother's record collection. Looking back in 1995, his views on the genre are less sympathetic than Tim's, merely viewing it as a stepping stone towards an appreciation of other, better styles: 'Heavy metal got me into music but then you mature and realise it's a load of crap. When I was even younger than that, my brother was into The Who and The Kinks and stuff like that. He brought those records home but I'm only kind of getting into them now.'

Rick had definitely moved on from his metallic roots and looked down his nose at terrible groups like Vietnam and their childish passions. By 1992, he too was developing a taste for the alternative music scene, including the ubiquitous Nirvana. When Tim and Mark first approached him to join their group, he was not exactly enthusiastic. If Rick had mixed feelings about them, Tim and Mark were equally dismissive of hiring this unprepossessing Adam Clayton lookalike. Tim's view was, 'He was just the geek who had just heard about us and he was the only drummer we knew, so we had to take him.' Mark was, characteristically, yet more dismissive. 'There wasn't anyone less likely to join a rock'n'roll band in the whole school but we were so desperate. I remember our first meeting. I felt suicidal even considering getting this geek in the band.' With a name selected at random out of a dictionary, Ash were formed.

2.

LUCK AND GOOD SONGS

It is one of life's sadder truisms that making it to the top takes a lot of hard work, attention to detail and a devotion to your chosen path. If you want to make it as a rock band, then however easy you make it look when you have got there, however casual your approach, however nonchalant your acceptance of fame and fortune, you will only be reaping the rewards due to you for putting in plenty of ground work, treading the boards in dismal venue after dismal venue on the toilet circuit, recording for weeks and months after hours of toil put into rehearsal upon rehearsal. Small wonder then that Ash's first demo tape was 'pretty grim' according to Tim, for the new three-piece band recorded it within a week or so of their formation, hardly time in which to strike up an instrumental empathy. For all Rick's obvious ability, it takes many long hours of rehearsal before any inexperienced drummer and bass player can turn themselves into a cohesive rhythm unit. The three were only too well aware of their failings, but decided to go ahead with their demo session anyway as it was already booked.

They had arranged to make their first recordings at Cosmic Rayz studio in the coastal town of Strangford, just a few miles from their Downpatrick homes. Uniquely, the studio had a seven-track recording desk, though this was of no real consequence to Ash at this early stage. Running through six songs which represented the best of the material Tim and Mark had pieced together back in the Wheeler bedroom, it was quickly apparent that while they had not reached any musical destination yet, they were moving fast on the right road. Most important of all, it was obvious that the three enjoyed working together and, hidden beneath the ragged collection of songs, there was that vital spark of intensity which marks out the very best bands from the run of the mill competition.

Tim gave a lot of the credit for their advance to Laser Gun Nun since, 'Through them we discovered The Ramones. I suppose they've really been our main role models. They showed us you can be loud and melodic and funny all at the same time.' There are few more cartoon-like bands than The Ramones, all taking the name of the brotherhood, clad in uniform shades and leather jackets, beanpole singer Joey Ramone cutting one of the most unlikely figures in rock'n'roll. On stage, starting almost every song with a cry of 'one two three four', they can seem faintly ridiculous with their heads down, start together and see you at the end, approach to their music. Yet their material has always been characterised by an uncanny ear for melody, their songs instantly memorable, catchy three-minute epics that combine classic 1960s pop songwriting with the frenetic attack of punk or thrash metal. The Ramones remain a sadly under-rated band, one who look like they stepped out of a DC comic book, but who have made a sizeable contribution to the music of the last twenty years. Ash's fascination with them was one of the first signs that here might be a band worthy of note.

Encouraged by this early venture into the studio and dreaming of emulating the brudders, rehearsals picked up pace. The summer holidays of 1992 were devoted to getting Ash up and running. They wrote new songs, practised them, played some early gigs. In short, they followed the routine that bands without number were running through all over the world. But this trio, only in their infancy, felt that they were good enough to break out of their home town, were arrogant enough to believe that they could make a go of things. The self belief that Tim felt was so crucial stood them in good stead. They desperately needed such fortitude for Downpatrick was distinctly underwhelmed by their efforts. If anything, this indifference lead the lads to redouble their efforts, their dedication fuelled by the constant reminder of the price of failure. Dwelling on his home town's attractions, Tim noted, 'work-wise there's a seat-belt factory and that is about it. We would probably have ended up going to college [if we hadn't had the band] but Rick's brother got a really good degree and the only job he's been able to find is in HMV. If you want to be earning more than £100 a week, then you've got no choice. You've got to go to the mainland.' If you feel you are eventually going to have to leave the comfort of your home town come what may, you might as well aim to be a rock star as an architect, might as well try to see all the world rather than just move to another anonymous town and live an anonymous life.

Throughout that summer, Ash, and Tim in particular, became prolific songwriters and by September they were ready to record a new batch of twelve songs. Going under the title *Garage Girl*, the selection featured the title track and others such as 'Solar Happy', 'Shed', 'Rick's Riff' and, most significantly, 'Jack Names The Planets'. This new material made it perfectly obvious that Ash had made a great leap forward. As both songwriters and performers, they clearly had a great deal of potential if only they could harness that ability consistently, focusing it in the right direction. 'Jack Names The Planets' in particular suggested that here was a band with all the right ingredients, and even allowing for their tender age, it is difficult to understand why no record company picked up on this particular song sooner than they did.

That twelve-track cassette did the rounds in their native Downpatrick, for the band put it on sale at their gigs. As a way of getting their name known and of raising a little extra money to fund their visits to the demo studios, it was excellent. Unfortunately, its distribution was almost purely local, the band sending copies to a mere handful of record companies who were thoroughly disinterested in it. Given that record company A&R executives rarely make the trek to Belfast, let alone Downpatrick, it was hardly surprising that Ash continued to languish in obscurity. In September 1992 Tim and Mark were still only fifteen and they found it even harder to get anyone within the music industry to take them seriously. If you wanted to make a record that featured school children, you called in a cutesie choir and provided them with a terrible schmaltzy song about the enchanting spectacle of grandma's false teeth, not a bunch of spotty adolescents out to make a row with their stories of desolation and the solar system. This was music business lore, writ large in the book of 'How To Make A Christmas Number One'.

Being stranded in Northern Ireland with no hope of getting a gig in London because of their age – they were so young that none of the capital's rock clubs would book them – their early enthusiasm for the band began to wane briefly. Tim may have been confident in his and the band's own talent but he was equally impatient with the inability of record companies to recognise it and was starting to fret about their future. In fairness, this was scarcely the industry's fault since Ash themselves have subsequently recognised their failure to go about things methodically or with any real sense of purpose. Looking back at that period which stretched on into the early months of 1993, Tim admitted, 'We didn't know how to get a record deal, we didn't even know how we were ever gonna get out of Downpatrick. We recorded some demos when we could and every bit of spare cash the three of us had was put into the band to try to get somewheres. Eventually we just worked our arses off. We played a few gigs in Belfast but there's not much of a scene where local bands can get to play. In the end we were getting pretty tired of it all.' The inevitable parental pressure, well-meaning but incredibly irritating, did little for Tim's state of mind either. 'They were always on at me to choose a proper career. They didn't take the band seriously as something we could make a living at so I spent years fending off questions about which university I was going to.'

It is possible to overstate the difficulties of being an Irish band when it comes to securing a record deal. Twenty or thirty years ago it was a real problem but since then a number of very successful bands have emerged, such that record companies do keep an eye on that part of the country. The fact that the Irish island has produced the likes of Van Morrison, Thin Lizzy, the Undertones, U2, Sinead O'Connor, Hothouse Flowers, Therapy? and The Cranberries makes it very obvious that companies ignore that talent pool at their peril. In addition, the long Irish literary tradition that has given us a host of wonderful writing over the last century and more further reinforces that view. The descendants of Joyce and Shaw must be worthy of scrutiny. However, in the past, the Irish have usually been forced to meet the British establishment half way, making the pilgrimage to London, either temporarily or, in many cases, permanently. Ash were different.

Circumstances conspired to keep them at home and yet by the summer of 1993, just as they were at their most disenchanted, salvation was at hand. Although they had approached just a few select record companies without success, their demo tapes were doing the rounds of the London companies as one A&R man passed it to another, who lent it to a record plugger who gave it a journalist who handed it to a sound man who. . .well, you get the picture. At the end of this game of pass the parcel, *Garage Girl* landed up in the offices of the Bad Moon public relations company. Bad Moon had already made a name for themselves with industry insiders, handling the press and publicity in the UK for bands such as Nirvana, the Beastie Boys, Carter USM and The Senseless Things. Given that Ash were already heavily influenced by Nirvana, this was a real break because Bad Moon were already predisposed to their kind of material. More fortunate still was the fact that in the office next door to Bad Moon's was Steve Taverner, who had previously run the independent label Big Cat Records.

Like many connected with the music business, Taverner was a sharp businessman but more importantly, he was a genuine music fan. He was struck by the potential that *Garage Girl* showcased and was intrigued by their surprising marriage of grinding grunge with a flair for pop melody. Listening to demo tapes is a difficult business; it requires a very special state of mind and an extremely discerning ear to weed out the very best material from stuff that is merely pleasant or enjoyable. Given the number of new singles turfed out each week, it takes something out of the ordinary to rise above the crowd. Taverner felt that Ash had that crucial ingredient. For him, this was a wonderful example of synchronicity, for he was in the process of setting up a new label, La La Land Records, and was looking for a flagship band to launch it. Suddenly that band had fallen into his lap, with 'Jack Names The Planets' the obvious choice as La La Land's first single.

If Taverner felt that he had been lucky in finding Ash, that was nothing compared with the amazement the band felt when Taverner contacted them. They had continued plugging away on the home front, playing gigs as and when they could, and claiming a reasonable reputation for themselves among the local cognoscenti, though even in Downpatrick, their prowess remained something of a well kept secret. A three-piece can be a difficult proposition on stage, for there is a tendency for them to be too static, rooted to their corner of the stage, draped around their instruments. Without a lead singer who is free to roam without any instrumental responsibilities, they can be a dull spectacle. Nirvana had shown that it was possible to rise above that and Chris Novoselic's whirling around the stage was clearly an inspiration for Mark's later antics. At this stage though, the stages they played were small ones and it was left to Mark to make his impact sartorially rather than physically. As Rick recalled, 'Mark was king of the fucked-up uniform. He used to wear this really chewed up tie done up backwards so only the skinny bit was showing. And he had this really holey jumper that he wore all the time.'

This live work had toughened up the Ash sound such that by the time Taverner – Tav as he was widely known – made his interest in them known, they were ready to make the most of the opportunity. Tim jumped at the chance, thankful that at last, Ash's time had come. 'It was just luck really. Luck and good songs. Put it down to fate. We kinda had this vision which we followed blindly for some reason and it's all gone pretty much according to plan. Somehow everything just fell into place. We were probably about to split up if we hadn't got that single out. So we might just have been boring A-level students if we hadn't got a record deal.'

Pretty much concurrent with Tav's interest in the band came Mark's own attempt to speed up the process. Like the other two, he was equally dispirited by their apparent inability to get anywhere and so he took it upon himself to help organise the release of a Northern Irish twelve-inch sampler EP, which featured Ash along with contemporaries Marabone, Fat and Buttlip. The EP, limited to a mere 500 copies, finally saw the light of day in October 1993 under the title *Raptor Presents* on Raptor records. Ash's contribution was a demo of 'Season', an affecting song that illustrated a different side of the band from that of 'Jack Names The Planets', making it an excellent section for the sampler. Ostensibly a simple metallic workout, the powerful guitar and driving rhythm track had the aggression of a band like Iron Maiden together with the grasp of dynamics that characterised the more sophisticated hard rock bands such as Rush. If these may sound like unappealing comparisons, just remember that the Nirvana sound was not all that far removed from that of noise metal – the greatest difference was one of attitude, of spirit and of execution. These disparate influences in themselves marked

'Season' down as something out of the ordinary, but there was still more to it than that. Termed a 'minor classic' by *Hot Press*'s Liam Fay, perhaps the most remarkable thing about the song was the lyrical maturity. Inspired by a teenage preoccupation with death and mortality, instead of the typically gory take that metal bands take on the subject, Tim's lyric was heartfelt and touching. He confessed later, 'I was going through a morbid period in 1994 and that is what happened, I wrote "Season" and "Jack Names The Planets" out of that feeling. People haven't seen the serious side of it. "Season" was meant to be about feelings of loss and missing someone and that was just the way I told the story. It is not based on truth but at the time I was into darker things.'

Tim's fascination with these deeper forces are quite typical of an evolving, enquiring mind. The teenage years provide the first time when we confront our own mortality, when we are expected to grow up and take on new responsibilities. The childhood simplicity of playing football, playing records and reading comics have to be set aside as we have to look towards getting the qualifications that will shape the rest of our lives – if you're a failure at sixteen, it takes a lot of effort to turn things around. With the pressures of school, of early relationships and of simple physiological change all having an impact, it is hardly surprising that so many teenagers flirt with suicidal ideas at some time, however briefly. Adolescence is a period where fiercely held ideals have yet to be diluted by experience and while adults often look back on their youthful selves with a mixture of embarrassment and loathing, that is a strange reaction. Our earlier years when we refuse to compromise are often when we are at our best, often when we are truest to our real selves, a time when we can experience emotions with a clarity and intensity of which the passage of time sometimes robs us. Perhaps that conflict was best described thus by Robert Smith of The Cure: 'You're forced to close down as you get older because you cannot break down on the factory floor because people think either you're a nutter or a nonce or something. You just cannot do it, but I think it is that pressure that forces people to give up ... when you're a teenager you're still able to express that kind of emotion and not feel embarrassed by it ... to me that is the idea of growing old, no longer being able to say what you really feel, always having to pretend that you're someone else ... I still despair when I look at the conventional world of adulthood.'

With their first song available to the public, perhaps it is time to look a little harder at Ash and make a few comparisons with other artists who have ploughed a similar furrow. On a musical level, a kinship with the likes of Nirvana, The Wedding Present, The Ramones and The Undertones has been suggested. It is true that there are similarities between Ash and the work of these other bands, but this is no more than is to be expected. Pick virtually any record by any band and you will the echoes of someone else in it. That is just the turning of the musical wheel. To find a truer picture of a band, their aims and motivations, it is necessary to dig a little deeper, to look for artists with whom they share an attitude, a state of mind. In that sense, Ash are reminiscent of no band more than The Cure. The Cure also started as a trio, featuring the classic guitar, bass, drums line-up. The Cure's main man is lead singer and guitarist Robert Smith, the man responsible for the majority of the group's songwriting. The Cure started with Smith still a schoolboy, their big break coming while studying for A-levels. Success came to them very young and in their earliest days, The Cure lived an incredibly hedonistic lifestyle, not only burning the candle at both ends but in the middle too, taking on board their fair share of drink and drugs. The Cure's Lol Tolhurst served as a punchbag, literally and metaphorically, a safety valve for the rest of the group's frustrations – Rick is similarly humiliated on a ritual basis, especially, though not exclusively by Mark, though thankfully not in such a vicious fashion as Tolhurst sometimes was. Like Ash, The Cure had no real idea how to find pop stardom, but chanced upon it when they saw an advert in *Melody Maker* asking 'Wanna be a recording star?' Their break was via a talent contest of sorts, record company Hansa attempting, unsuccessfully, to sign them up as a consequence. The Cure then found a former A&R man, Chris Parry, looking to set up his own label, Fiction. These parallels are striking, but relatively superficial.

What does suggest similarities of a deeper nature is the approach. Robert Smith was and, to an extent, remains a control freak. He oversees every aspect of The Cure's recording career from the broadest brush to the finest detail. Tim Wheeler fills a similar Fuhrer-like role with Ash.

Nothing escapes his attention and it is his approach to life and his view of the wider picture, his ambitions for his career that informs their music most clearly of all. Smith formed The Cure to escape from ordinary life and it was this fierce desire that was Tim's prime motivation in starting a band – recall his comment that he wanted more from life than the seemingly inevitable cycle of school-university-dead-end job-retirement-death, that it was about 'not being conventional, not fitting in with society, being free'. Smith has regularly pointed out that he would rather kill himself than do an ordinary nine-to-five job.

On another front, Smith's lyrics are all about loss, desolation, the inexorable passing of time and the effect on relationships. His musical approach to the subjects can be funereal as on 'Faith' or joyously psychotic as on 'Kiss Me Kiss Me Kiss Me'. In addition, Smith is a master of pure popcore, the early classic 'Boys Don't Cry' being a glorious example of Buzzcocks-inspired idiot pop, essential new wave, economical and direct. A predecessor of 'Jack Names The Planets', in fact, but a mere example of the diversity of their taste and talents. Ash have shown similar qualities in their early days to suggest that they can challenge The Cure for longevity, quality and diversity, but only time can provide a definitive answer.

Just as the release of 'Season' had whetted a few appetites, it was time for Ash to capitalise upon the heightened curiosity of the rock fraternity. With £300 provided by Tav, they were set to record their début single at the tail end of

1993. They entered Nova Tech Studios in Belfast, a considerably more advanced studio than Cosmic Rayz in Strangford, to record 'Jack Names The Planets' and its B-side, 'Don't Know'. Assisted by engineer Gary Aitken, the band were less than enthralled with the results. Used to their aggressive, harsh and extremely rowdy on-stage sound, one which they carried over into rehearsals too, they were surprised by the restrained nature of the finished product. Tim told *Record Collector*, 'It didn't represent how we sounded at that time. The production is quite primitive and it was a lot cleaner than we wanted it to be. Mark in particular didn't like it. "Don't Know" is really good, though.'

It is worth remembering that 'Jack Names The Planets' had already been around in the Ash canon for more than a year before they cut it as a single. It had found its way on to the *Garage Girl* demo that Tav so admired in September 1992 but now, in the twilight of 1993, it was old news. As so often happens with songs that are played time and again, they go through many changes, live performance tending to make them both faster and rougher, by accident rather than design. Also, as perhaps their best song to this point, during the few local concerts they played, they would attack it with relish, the adrenaline of live performance pounding it into a very different shape. This was not what Tav was looking for. He was interested in the simple pop dynamics that had been apparent on its earliest incarnation, looking to play up its power pop potential, to make the most of the Nirvana constructed pop world of the time. To simply try to be louder and more powerful than the likes of Nirvana or Pearl Jam was to invite failure, to ghettoise a band that would always find its greatest success by concentrating on its artful tunefulness. Not only that, but the Sound of Seattle was seen as being men's music, performed by aggressive types like Mudhoney, Tad, Nirvana themselves, Soundgarden and so on. In the first example of age discrimination they would face, it was also unlikely that followers of the heavy end of the grunge spectrum would take kindly to its being played by a bunch of school kids. So the studio version of 'Jack Names The Planets' played up the pop dynamics to the detriment of the noisy, grungy guitars.

This moving tale was based on 'The Talisman' by Stephen King according to Tim. 'My parents are both alive, but this song was really about missing someone and knowing that they have to go. The concept of separation has always appealed to me.' Yet if it illustrated his facility with words, it reinforced all their musical credentials still further. The song was a mass of different influences, its slacker approach recalling Dinosaur Jr, the guitar harmonics coming from the U2 songbook, the sub-science fiction metaphor from The Pixies via their love of The Beach Boys' California surfing sound, Tim's deadpan vocal akin to that of The Buzzcocks' Pete Shelley. What could have been a horrible mish-mash of stolen ideas actually came out as a solidly worked through concoction of influenced originality. Ash were already good enough on this showing to absorb other people's ideas and not simply regurgitate them.

The single was unleashed in February 1994 in a limited run of just 1,000 copies, though a further 2,000 were quickly pressed up in the wake of its success. Writing in Dublin's *Hot Press*, Lorraine Feeney called it 'simply delicious': 'It's short, it buzzes and you know that you're hearing something precious from the first listen. It's fun and God knows there are few enough fun records around these days.' Almost a year later, the *NME*'s Lisa Hoftijzer called it, 'Old, yet somehow young as love. Heartbreak and confusion were never this sweet. Or hopeless.' If those voices of approval were not enough testament of their burgeoning talent, it was yet more significant that Radio 1's then late-night DJ Mark Radcliffe played the single almost to the point of destruction on his influential programme, creating a real buzz of anticipation around the band. The big time was just around the corner.

3.

TOTAL CONTROL

As 1993 came to its close, Tim and Mark were involved in the early part of their A-level studies – Tim doing French, Maths and English, Mark following Art and Economic Studies – while Rick was readying himself to take his exams in History, Politics and English the following summer. Just as this was going on, they were embarking on a potentially successful career in the music world. Leading such a schizophrenic existence, they could be forgiven for throwing up their hands in frustration, kicking their academic studies into touch and embarking on a frenzied burst of rock'n'roll living. Instead, and showing remarkable maturity given the temptations that were on offer, they decided to pursue their scholastic ambitions. Tim pointed out at the time, 'I don't want to make the mistake of rushing into a band full time because it could all fall through at any minute.'

That was a perfectly reasonable attitude in the early months of 1994. Even though the 'Jack Names The Planets' single was causing a stir, Ash were hardly piling up the column inches in the press and nor were they getting much exposure on radio, Mark Radcliffe aside. In 1994 the focus was very much on bands like Elastica or Blur, the early rumblings of the Britpop scene, and the spurious New Wave of New Wave, a movement that was supposedly the mother of the rebirth of punk rock, spearheaded by the likes of S*M*A*S*H. Early that year Ash were treated as a novelty school group if they were mentioned at all, something which acted quite decisively to their advantage. If their early adventures in the recording studio had been promising, one single was not enough to build a career upon. That first single had been a good start, offering firm foundations, but Ash had a lot of work to do if they were going to make the leap from being a decent amateur band to a thoroughly good professional one. Away from the public eye in the secluded Downpatrick environment, the trio kept plugging away in rehearsals, furthering their songwriting and performing ambitions, gradually honing and improving their act.

Nevertheless, there were opportunities to dip a toe in the water and take a closer look at what they would be getting themselves into if the band became a full-time occupation. In the Easter holidays, in the first week of April 1994, Ash played their first shows on the UK mainland, a six-date tour giving them the opportunity to play in front of the nation's record companies. It was obvious that La La Land was not going to be a permanent home for the band for it would never have the clout to promote and distribute their records in the way they would require if they were to fulfil their dreams of chart domination, dreams they shared with Tav who was now their manager. Tim describes Tav as 'knowing everyone there is to know in the industry', and so he was clearly a useful man to have on your side, particularly if, like Ash, you knew virtually nothing about the said industry.

The early dates did not go off without a hitch. Heading off to Scunthorpe, Ash played a typically rough and ready venue, only to find themselves broke at the end of the night. Mark recalled in *Melody Maker*, 'The promoter wouldn't pay us at the end of the gig so we had to threaten him with his life. Eventually we got the money off his mum. We went round to her house in the middle of the night and made her write us a cheque. The guy was in tears.' The picture of Ash as rock'n'roll hoodlums so early on is not an altogether convincing one, but it is one that Mark was keen to perpetuate, sometimes to his detriment. Later for instance, he told *Q*'s Howard Johnson that Ash had been running a scam at their high school of which the Mafia would have been proud: 'We had a deal going with the guy in the school tuck shop. He'd give us two or three quids worth of sweets and a fiver in change every day. Over the course of a year or more, more than a grand went missing and it was a really big deal, the police were called in and everything. We had to deny all knowledge.' Once faced with his words in cold, hard print, Mark could not retract it quickly enough, telling *Hot Press*, 'When that tuck shop story appeared, my parents hated the idea of everybody thinking I'm a thief, which I'm not. In the end, they phoned the head master and he said, "Don't worry, I know it's a load of bollocks".'

Once more, Mark's airheaded ability to act before he had put his mind in gear had landed him in trouble; when your every word is reported in the press, you need to take more care than Mark had hitherto managed. For example, he probably regrets the following outburst too: 'We nicked an overhead projector from school. We threw it over the wall and smashed it to bits. I could go on for hours about vandalism. Vandalism is brilliant, especially when you're with your friends. There is such a heavy police presence in Downpatrick that there is a really good chance of getting caught, so when you do it and run off, there is a real adrenalin rush.' If these were true stories, then given his later behaviour with Ash, Mark's addiction to the 'adrenalin rush' is a potentially destructive aspect of his character that needs careful handling. Having said that, on the publication of these tales, there were further strenuous denials in the local Belfast press. If those denials were accurate, it is clear that there is nothing intentionally nasty or malicious in his actions, but they were just part of a seemingly lifelong determination to live the rock'n'roll life to the full, embellishing, exaggerating and inventing as he went along. He pointed that out with the easy way he took to the rigours and depravations of touring, right from the outset: 'I loved it. Sleeping on top of your amps in the back of a transit van is brilliant!' Rather than a thug, it would be closer to the truth to describe Mark as being daft as a brush and leave it at that.

Among those earliest shows was a crucial gig at the Powerhaus in London's Islington. Inviting all and sundry to see his new charges, Tav's enterprise worked by way of a rave review from the *NME*'s Angela Lewis. Discussing Tim's lack of experience, she wrote, 'Tim's an awkward mover and not a brilliant singer but guitar in tow, he has a spark way beyond his years. Behind the deceptively shy smile and off-key hollers is a demon in waiting, out to etch his name on the indie upstart wall of acclaim.' Positive though it was, in a sense the review missed the point for labelling Ash as another indie band was to underestimate the level and intensity of their aspirations and the strength of their belief in themselves and their songs. They had no desire to follow the same career curve as bands like Mega City Four, The Senseless Things, Pop Will Eat Itself or The Wonder Stuff, becoming darlings of the press and the college circuit, scoring a couple of hit singles in this country but meaning nothing to anyone beyond these shores, and eventually collapsing beneath the weight of stymied ambition.

Perhaps aiming for the heights is a function of coming from beyond the mainland, perhaps simply from being outside England. If any English band starts to cast its net beyond these shores, the press are very quick to slap them down, to accuse them of suffering delusions of grandeur, to try to keep them in their place. This has been so for such a long time that English bands have grown ever more comfortable within the confines of this country, happy to cultivate a cult following that will deliver a decent showing for each new single and album in the first week of sale but which aims no higher than that. It is just not cool to want to be a massive success, though perhaps Oasis are starting to change that perception at last. If you look at bands like U2 from Ireland or Simple Minds from Scotland however, they have not suffered from that particular hang-up. Their raison d'être has always been to take their music to as many people as possible. If they are writing what they feel to be good songs, then it is only sensible to expose those songs to as many people as they possibly can. If that means selling a lot of records in the process, then so be it – they were not going to be embarrassed by that aspect of their success. It is certainly a very pleasurable by-product and while they may have lain themselves open to criticism for being populist, those jibes dissolved once the band realised that could walk out on to a stage and perform before 75,000 die-hard fans in virtually any country in the world. Ash are certainly happier to follow the U2 rather than the Echo & the Bunnymen model. Mark was clear about his response to that kind of élitism: 'We want to be successful everywhere.'

Angela Lewis's review continued in euphoric vein: 'These Belfast teen kickers aren't revolution babes – if they carried the weight of the world on their shoulders, "Jack Names The Planets" couldn't soar so high. At present Ash possess a whiff of earth magic to send songs roaring down the fast lane in the dynamics department.' In spite of such a rapturous response from one of music's more influential organs, the record companies did not exactly beat a path to Ash's Downpatrick door. Even an appearance on Channel

4's late night music show *Naked City* and an acclaimed session for John Peel's Radio 1 show failed to have much impact, though their choice of songs left a little to be desired. Ash played their own 'Petrol' and 'Season', but also performed 'Silver Surfer', a song by Backwater, the latest incarnation of the influential Laser Gun Nun. Bringing their friends and mentors to the attention of the nation was a nice gesture, but on a personal level they would have been better served by playing all original material. Even so, it is hard to criticise anyone too much for being loyal to their friends.

In the end it was of little account, for with the Easter holidays at an end they had work to do. Returning to Downpatrick without having inked a deal was not the end of the world for almost immediately Infectious Records made their interest in Ash perfectly clear. Infectious seemed to be an ideal home for a band like Ash, one coming from the heart of the independent sector but with its eyes on far wider success. Infectious was run by Korda Marshall, the man who had signed The Eurythmics at RCA and who had worked with bands like Pop Will Eat Itself during his time with that label. With those sort of credentials to back him up, he quickly endeared himself to Ash and they were more than happy to do business with him. To their credit, Ash were in no rush to jump into bed with the label even though it was the only one showing an interest in them, and their recording contract was not finally signed until July 1994. As Tim pointed out, We wanted to get to do exactly what we wanted – to have control over the records, to go to university if we wanted to. Infectious gave us all that.'

Continuing with their studies at university was still a possibility at this stage. After all, they had yet to release a single on a proper national scale and who was to say that anyone would be interested in that? If they were quickly exposed as flops, then university might suddenly look a whole lot more attractive. With that in mind, they buckled down to the last few weeks of the school term, with Rick approaching his final exams. Even then, the on-going story of his band loomed large. All his teachers fully anticipated him passing with flying colours and so conversation turned to his next step. With Tim and Mark consigned to a further full year in the education system, Rick needed to decide where he would spend his next twelve months, with a university place the obvious choice. The next question was where to study. With his two colleagues trapped in Downpatrick, he could hardly go to the mainland and retain his place in the group and so the choice was considerably narrower than it might have been. He remembered, 'Our headmaster asked me why I wanted to go to university in Belfast so I told him it was because I was in a band. He asked me which one and when I told him, he said "Ash? Oh, I've heard they're excellent!"' This was not the only compliment that he received from the halls of academe, for he also recalled that his history teacher told him that his daughter had their poster on her wall. Their continuing schooldays had a generally beneficial effect on the band, certainly on Tim and Rick who were quite content to remain in that environment, Tim even crediting his English teacher with changing their musical direction. 'We were the sort who actually got on our with our teachers,' said Tim. Unsurprisingly, Mark was a little less sanguine, straining at the leash, keen to get back on the road, back into the studio, back into the band.

With Rick's exams put of the way – three straight As accomplished with ease and, according to his version of events, a minimum of revision – Ash could throw themselves back into their alternative career, at least for the duration of the summer. The first manifestation of this freedom came with two gigs in one day in London in June. Having played at the annual Fleadh Festival in Finsbury Park in the afternoon – a gig which 'suffered' when the band turned up officially 'legless' according to a story in *Hot Press* – they next surfaced at the Splash club in King's Cross to a warm reception, indicating that their star was definitely in the ascendant. June was a pretty hectic month since in the midst of their 'school's out' euphoria, Rick suffered a nasty car accident and Tim was left stranded on a mountain for six hours! Such accident prone behaviour aside though, these were exciting times for the band for they were ready to cut their first single under the Infectious deal. In spite of some suggestions that it might be wise to rework 'Jack Names The Planets', the band were determined to choose a new song, recording 'Petrol' for release on CD and an extremely limited seven-inch vinyl pressing of just 500 copies. Evidence of their increased status came with the engagement of Mark Waterman, an established and highly successful producer with both Ride and Elastica, to pilot them through this crucial period.

Waterman's greater experience was quickly evident on this new single, helping Ash fully realise their pop sound within their chosen punky framework. The band were rightly pleased with their labours, even though Mark summed up the B-sides, 'The Little Pond' and 'Things' with the succinct phrase 'They're crap!' Nevertheless, it was 'Petrol' that interested the audience most and that was a clear success. The chiming guitar introduction was both welcoming and anthemic, the sudden change of pace intriguing, Tim's still thin vocals allowed to reach out from the sound rather than being hidden in the mix. It was with 'Petrol' that the first comparisons with The Undertones came to the fore, something that was to irritate for some time. Yet there was a striking, if superficial similarity, Tim's voice sounding uncannily like Feargal Sharkey on this occasion. Looking beyond that, the frenzied guitar was more reminiscent of The Cure, the solid sheet of sound providing the same uncompromising attack as that of The Wedding Present, *NME*'s Lisa Hotijzer remarking on 'an explosion of Kennedy-like guitars', a perfectly valid reference point.

On the single's release in August 1994, *Hot Press*'s Gerry McGovern felt that 'Petrol' 'shows they can knock up powerful slices of pop. Right now though they're skimming a pot where a thousand indie bands have rightly sunk into oblivion. Can they rise above?' That hint of scepticism was an important addition to the debate, for the world of indie-pop had a habit of throwing up bands who could charm with early singles before descending into creative atrophy in a matter of months. For Ash to make their mark, they would need to do more than simply ape the sound of a phalanx of guitar-jangling, flop-fringed failures.

With that in mind, perhaps the most interesting review of 'Petrol' came from Andy Cairns of Therapy?, guest reviewer in *Melody Maker*. He was the first to notice the more experimental, adventurous side to Ash's muse, an element that could easily be overlooked under their wall of sound. Cairns pointed out, 'What's really great about this is that it's people experimenting a bit more than the usual boring 4-4 formats. This is the sound of confused young Belfast. The singer's a really good songwriter. It gets better every time I hear it. It all just soars.' This intervention from Therapy?, albeit in such a small way, is nonetheless significant, for it demonstrates just how often fate has taken a helping hand in the Ash story.

Even the band concede that, good songs or not, they were lucky to get their vital introduction to Steve Taverner, an introduction which paved the way towards eventual success. Once they were up and running as a recording band, fortune continued to smile on them. Not only did they have the right contacts, but they came out of Northern Ireland at a time when a number of other bands there were establishing a musical scene worthy of note, one which enticed regular reporters over to Belfast to check out what was happening. With Northern Ireland just feeling the benefits which attended the cessation of violence from both loyalist and republican paramilitaries, it was no longer such a forbidding place for the mainlanders. Amongst its own people, the end to hostilities, however temporary, was a reason for celebration and a good excuse to have a party. Feeding off this changing mood, bands such as Therapy?, Scheer, Chimera and their long-time rivals Backwater were reaping a harvest of interest. It was into this very healthy situation that Ash emerged in the summer of 1994.

It is very easy to be dismissive of 'scenes' and 'movements' within the music industry but they can be incredibly helpful in getting bands noticed and off the ground. If, for example, you take something like the Madchester explosion of 1989, a whole host of bands had their fifteen minutes of fame purely because they lived in the same corner of England as The Stone Roses and The Happy Mondays. A journalist may be despatched to the centre of this burgeoning new scene in order to file a story on the leaders and while there may chance upon a new band, either by seeing them in a dingy club, maybe as a support band or perhaps by virtue of a chance remark during the course of an interview or from a roadie with whom he might be sharing a drink. In that way, a band that might otherwise wait weeks, months or years for the oxygen of publicity to come their way can suddenly be elevated to the pages of the press without having to slog around the country in search of fans. Of course, once you have the publicity, you then have to justify your fame by delivering the goods and it is equally advisable to detach yourselves from a scene that will inevitably die a quick death when the circle of fashion moves on – look back at the countless careers ended by an association with the shoegazing phenomenon for example. Rick was already wise to the dangers when, having escaped the clutches of any Belfast movement, journalists tried to lump Ash in with the New Wave of New Wave: 'We've heard all about the NWONW and from the sound of things, we could probably fit in with all of that but we've not actually heard any of the new bands, let alone the old ones! To be honest, we'd rather be seen as something independent of that.'

This was a sensible policy, but the explanation was surely disingenuous at best. To say that they knew nothing of the punk bands of the 1970s was ridiculous, particularly since they had been so inspired by Laser Gun Nun, through whom they had discovered The Ramones. Equally, Tim was dismissive of any comparisons with earlier Northern Irish alumni The Undertones. While it was lazy to bunch the two bands together just because they came from the same part of the world – you might as well say that Take That sound like The Smiths just because they were from Manchester – there was a resemblance. It may simply have been down to the accent and the very Irish rhythms of their speech, giving Tim and Feargal Sharkey a similar tone at times, but Tim would have none of that. Instead, he offered a kind of scorched earth policy, suggesting that Ash were their own men and had learned nothing from those who had come before: 'The Undertones comparison is really strange. I suppose it's something to do with the fact that we're both from Northern Ireland so people assume there is a connection. But Derry is a long way from County Down. I'm the only one of the three of us who's even heard any of their records and I've only heard a couple of their songs.' Given that 'Teenage Kicks' is one of the anthems of the punk anthem, that The Undertones scored a number of hit singles that are still played regularly at indie clubs and even on the radio and that That Petrol Emotion, the band formed from the ashes of The Undertones continued to do well right throughout the 1980s and were a constant presence on the musical scene, it is hard to see just how Ash could have avoided hearing them. To do so, and to draw something from them was no crime, just as it was not a sin to be inspired by The Buzzcocks or Dinosaur Jr for 'Jack Names The Planets'. Presumably Tim's vituperative reaction to The Undertones connection was designed to prevent Ash being ghettoised as Northern Irish musicians, forced into singing about the troubles and life on the streets of Belfast. If so, it was unnecessary for it was their youth that pricked most people's curiosity, not their nationality.

With 'Petrol' ready for release, the band set off on their most extensive tour to date to promote it. It was a tour which would change attitudes towards Ash forever, both inside and outside the group. As Mark pointed out, 'That's when things really kicked off. It was proper insanity because everyone was together all the time.'

4.

PROPER INSANITY

The start of Ash's inexorable rise to the top, towards number one albums and top-ten singles, can really be traced back to August 1994. That was when the touring began in earnest, the time when they started to build up an intensely loyal fan base. It saw the release of their Infectious début to no little acclaim. It was the period when Ash first stuck a tentative toe into the waters of full-on rock'n'roll living. It was the time when Rick began to cultivate his reputation as an international-class boozer and butt of his band mates' practical jokes, the time when Mark began his descent into a potentially crippling illness.

August provided them with a chance to criss-cross the UK and Ireland at breakneck speed, packing in as much touring into as short a time as possible before school reeled them back in again. In hindsight, it might not have been the greatest idea. Going on tour, particularly as a small band playing tiny venues on a shoestring budget, is a bit of a culture shock to put it mildly. While it may be exciting to be let off the leash, to be away from home with the licence to do anything you want to do – the more so at the age of seventeen or eighteen – it is a lifestyle to which you have to adapt gradually. If you throw yourself into the whole thing with utter abandon and no regard for pacing yourself over the course of a tour, the results can be frightening.

This first tour was comparatively short and, given that the three were young, fit and healthy, they were able to lose themselves in the thrill of being on the road, coming out the other side in September relatively unscathed. Nevertheless, they set themselves a dangerous precedent with their reckless behaviour. Mark admitted, 'On stage, it's my job to run around and get the audience going but away from that, I'm probably the most irresponsible out of all of us. Especially on tour – I can be a nightmare. The tour manager practically has to be a parent to me. I'm rubbish.' Though that might be an honest self-appraisal, it did little to change his attitude.

On and off stage, the August gigs were a riotous success. Tim noted the changing nature of the audience and the vaguely hysterical reaction they were starting to get: 'Our gigs are always packed with weirdos now, doing a dance called the Pylon, where you jump on a big pile of bodies and beat shit out of each other. It's wild. Somebody broke his leg doing that!' *Melody Maker*'s Ian Watson, surveying the carnage at a gig at Belfast's Limelight, noted that the band 'display natural confidence. They may only have an average age of eighteen, but this Downpatrick trio clearly believe they were born to whip their peers into a delirious sweat sodden frenzy and judging by the past reaction of their fans (the local intensive care unit is put on stand-by whenever they play) they are probably right.' It was no surprise that their gigs should attract such madness for they invited it with the aggression they showed on stage, combining the pop attack of their early singles with the noisy, industrial, grinding grunge of other material such as 'Obscure Thing' which conjured up visions of Nine Inch Nails. At that same Limelight gig, Tim dished out such vicious treatment to his instrument that within a few minutes, he had trashed two guitars, their strings slashed by the ferocity of his attack on them. It was not always wise to mete out such treatment, for he only had the two guitars at the time, and on this particular occasion had to borrow another from the support band, Backwater. Nevertheless, it was a telling insight into the manic way they approached each show.

Already Ash were making a lot of noise within the belly of the rock industry, with bands such as Ride offering support slots. They were not the first to do so, Ash having turned down earlier offers from Daisy Chainsaw and the Frank & Walters because of school commitments. Ride's offer came through at the right time. In addition, they possessed the right degree of credibility, had the right links – having been produced by Mark Waterman – and offered a short cut through to the right audience.

Another memorable support slot came in August when they travelled with Babes In Toyland. *Hot Press*'s Gerry McGovern caught one of those shows and opined, 'The lead singer gave the impression that he wished he was anywhere except up on stage. It was hard to be impressed by such a lacklustre performance.' Certainly working with the Babes could be a scary, daunting experience and it must have been tough to make an impression on a crowd so committed to the headliners, but McGovern's verdict was a minority opinion. Babes In Toyland themselves became Ash devotees and their hard-core audience took to the young Irishmen with equal fervour.

Perhaps understandably, the Northern Irish press was a little more suspicious of Ash's meteoric rise to prominence than their London-based counterparts. After all, Ash had not paid their dues, had not racked up hundreds of shows in and around Belfast. *NME*'s Simon Williams caught the mood in his review of the gig at the Limelight: 'In one Belfast paper, a hack even has the gall to tut-tut about the recent attention afforded Ash, basically saying "They're good, but hey, come on guys, they're not *that* good, right?"' Williams himself could not agree with such a condescending view, being wildly enthusiastic in his endorsement of the band: 'Ash embody a nascent sense of chaos, wrecked guitars and all. And parts of this show splutter along, redeemed only by the incessant attentions of the moshpit. Ash plunder a promisingly deep shaft of creativity – [they] stand for the sound of youth like very few others.'

It was perfectly true to say that Ash were wildly inconsistent at this point, but then they had only been together for just on two years, writing and rehearsing pretty much in their spare time, rather than treating the band as a full-time job. It was inevitable there would be rough edges, that some songs would hit while others missed. As songwriters, they were still in their infancy, trying to master that most difficult of arts. Their on-stage power served to mask the faults for an audience out for a good time pure and simple, but the band themselves were not blind to their shortcomings. With that in mind, possibly it was just as well that they still had school to go back to, that it was possible for them to duck out of the limelight for a while, get back to normal life and work the songs through some more. If Ash was to be a long-term project, it would stand or fall by the quality of the material and as yet, there were not enough good songs to go round.

Playing live on a regular basis toughened up their sound though, giving a menacing edge to songs that might otherwise have seemed lightweight. Ian Watson summed up the value of their live work when he noted, 'Their surreal but carefree lyrics take on a nasty edge. Forget teenage kicks. Ash dispense teenage kickings.' Such aggression was, paradoxically, a source of both strength and weakness. By concentrating on unbridled noise as opposed to controlled power, they were likely to produce material that sagged. Where 'Petrol' would soar on a bright melody and an impressive grasp of songwriting dynamics, 'Obscure Thing' would flounder beneath the weight of macho posturing, an attempt to say that though they might be teenagers, they could be as tough as Mudhoney. It simply failed to convince and though songs such as that stayed in their act for some time, it was really a case of back to the drawing board.

It was back to the blackboard too come September, a

situation that brought conflicting emotions to the surface. For Rick, it was a difficult and slightly surreal period. Signing up to Queen's University in the heart of Belfast was the obvious route for him to take, but in truth he was doing little more than treading water for a year until his comrades had finished with their A-level studies. The gigs throughout the summer had gone so well that he was sure that Ash would become a full time job by the following year. Consequently, he found it tough to fully commit himself to his studies, in the almost certain knowledge that he would drop out after his first year. Without that determination to study, the degree syllabus which comprised lectures in social anthropology, politics and history soon lost whatever appeal it might have once held. Had he moved into a student bedsit or halls of residence straight away, he might have been able to spend months without rising from his pit, but initially at least he had to commute to Belfast from his Downpatick base. 'When I started at university I was still living at home and my dad gave me a lift in every morning. I couldn't get out of it so I ended up in Belfast and just skipped the lectures after I got there.' On the occasions when he did manage to attend, his levels of concentration were not all they might have been: 'I went to a lecture completely pissed once. It was brilliant. It was the only time I ever understood what my social anthropology lecturer was going on about.'

While Rick was living a fairly carefree existence, Tim was perfectly happy to return to school, surprisingly positive about the change of pace and of scenery which it offered. Perhaps school provided him with a refuge from the increasing burdens that were being placed upon him. As lead singer, front-man, main songwriter and group spokesman, a lot was expected of Tim Wheeler. The onset of fame at any age can be daunting, but as a seventeen-year-old who had arrived from nowhere, and one who was suddenly expected to be able to dispense nuggets of philosophy on the meaning of life to an assembled throng of pressmen at the drop of a hat, the anonymity of school life clearly had its attractions. And in Downpatrick, he remained surprisingly anonymous, for few of their contemporaries were interested in the band. Since signing to Infectious, their gigs had all been played out way beyond the confines of Downpatrick and so few people back home knew of their success. Tim deliberately chose to keep things that way, pointing out, 'In the beginning we kept quiet about playing gigs because we knew it would get us into trouble but you can hardly appear on *Top Of The Pops* or something and say, "No, that's only someone who looks like us!" ' Even so, in the confines of the classroom, Tim was able to revel in the joys of being one of the crowd and not the focus of attention, the one who had to entertain everyone.

Just as importantly, by regularly dropping back into the shadows, Ash were not risking over-exposure and nor were they being expected to carry the torch for independent music against the corporate rock beast. Tim admitted, 'Being in a position where we haven't been able to do too much too soon [because of school] has helped. The pressure that a band like Elastica are under to be the best band in the world is ridiculous. There's no way when you're only one album old and are still learning your trade that you can live up to those sort of expectations.' As he realised, Ash were a long way from being the finished article and needed time to grow up musically away from the public gaze, to make their mistakes in the rehearsal room, not in full view of the nation's press at a showcase gig in London. He made the sensible point, 'It's actually quite good being at school because you have a lot more time off and long holidays when you can practice. There's probably more free time than there would be if we were working in the band full-time.'

Tim did not use school simply as a means of escape though as he genuinely wanted to finish his exams and obtain the best grades possible. After all, who knew whether or not he might need to fall back on them some time in the future. In that light, Ash was almost a distraction he could do without: 'My teachers were worried and I knew that I didn't have Rick's natural intelligence. So [when we came back in September 1994] I decided I wouldn't do any more gigs while we were supposed to be at school. Then we got a call from Elastica . . ."

In the autumn of 1994, there was no more exciting nor widely touted band than Elastica, charismatically lead by Justine Frischmann. Heavily influenced by the New Wave – as their legal entanglements with Wire and The Stranglers made very clear – they were the ideal band for Ash to work with, the more so given their association with Elastica's producer Mark Waterman. The opportunity to work with them at close hand and to expose their own music to Elastica's audience, a crowd already predisposed towards new wave and primed for Ash's sound, was far too good an opportunity to miss. The biggest problem was one of timing. Elastica were scheduled to be on the road throughout October, right in the midst of the school term. As Tim had pointed out, there were worries that the time he was giving to Ash was detracting from his studies and so there was some stiff opposition to his desire to go on the road for the best part of a month. Initially, the headmaster made it clear that there was no way he would allow them the time off and that should be the end of the matter.

Had things not moved on from this impasse, then the consequences could have been very serious. With Mark not altogether happy at school anyway, he would surely have pushed for the band leaving and going on tour. Given his very relaxed attitude to university, Rick had no problems missing lectures either, so the pressure would have been on Tim. At such an early stage of their development, who knows whether or not it might have even split the band. Tim was determined to complete his A-levels and so might have chosen to go on with his studies, provoking resentment among the other two, however well they might have disguised it. Alternatively, if Tim had buckled and quit school altogether, he might have remained bitter at being forced into such a corner, creating a rift in the band. It is worthwhile remembering that a trio is the most potentially volatile of units, lending itself to two-versus-one arguments all the time, leaving one person isolated. Paradoxically, it takes more work to keep a three-piece together than a larger band, where initially you might think there is more opportunity for disagreement. With a four- or five-piece set-up, at least one person is seldom out on a limb, with most willing or able to fall in with one clique or another – if they fail to do so, they are pretty quickly out of the door.

With the Elastica tour looming and a decision needed quickly, they represented an irresistible force coming up against the immovable object of headmasterly disapproval. In their desperation to solve the problem, Ash called in Steve Taverner in an attempt to broker some kind of agreement. Tav turned up at the school and, having had to wait outside the headmaster's office for half an hour, he proceeded to argue their case. Stressing the career enhancing nature of the Elastica tour and arguing that he and the tour manager would always be on hand to keep an eye on these youthful charges, he gradually swung things in their favour. Whether the school were taken in by these blandishments is pretty unlikely because any teacher worth his salt will realise that his A-level students have moved a long way beyond the angelic stage. Surely the clinching factor in his allowing their release was that their parents were happy to see them go, their attitudes having shifted a little, as Tim explained, 'When we weren't getting anywhere our parents just thought it was stupid and that we should be concentrating on our studies. Now they're really pleased with us and show the CDs off to visitors!' If their parents said they could go, there was, in practice, little any headmaster could do to stop them. His delaying tactics were surely designed to try to get Tim and Mark to buckle down to their studies in advance of their departure. Indeed, Tim even made the promise that he would get down to some serious cramming while they were on the road, but then the road to hell is paved with good intentions. He had to admit, 'I took my books with me and managed half an hour of French in the van on the first night. Then I thought, "Sod this! Let's get pissed!"'

The Elastica tour introduced to the band to a new audience and coincided with a real whirl of activity. In September, Ash contributed a cover version of Helen Love's 'Punk Boy' to the Fierce Panda sampler EP *Crazed And Confused*, sub-titled 'Six Slabs of Adolescent Lunacy'. The track made their Ramones roots very obvious and it was perhaps the stand-out performance on the collection. This was no mean feat given the company – Supergrass, Credit To The Nation, Noise Addict, Gorky's Zygotic Mynci and Tribute To Nothing. A useful guide to new bands, *Crazy And Confused* did fall into cliché with its packaging, one child's T-shirt emblazoned with the legend 'Eat Your Parents'. Such dumb sloganeering surely belonged to another, more stupid era and scarcely reflected Ash's sentiments – they were continuing with their studies as much to please their parents as themselves after all.

More important than the EP was the October release of Ash's next Infectious single, 'Uncle Pat', issued to capitalise on the Elastica gigs. Although Tim later dismissed the song as 'the only vaguely Celtic thing we have done, and that was a piss-take', it offered another side of the band to the public, the reflective nature of the verses emphasising their diversity. Obviously anthemic in structure, it was the most atypical thing they had done to date, owing a little to the mid-1980s school of Big Country/Simple Minds/The Alarm, a big, dramatic track that sounded especially strong on radio, a little less so on the home hi-fi. Lyrically, it carried on with the theme established by 'Jack Names The Planets', Tim conceding '"Uncle Pat" is about missing someone.' Because of the pressures of time on Mark Waterman, and also so that Ash could try working with other people, 'Different Today', the B-side was mixed by David Gedge, leader of The Wedding Present, an obvious influence shown by the dense guitar sound.

Once again, Ash made a conscious decision to cater to the collector's market, not only issuing the single on the obligatory compact disc format, but as a limited edition, numbered seven-inch single, with a pressing of 1,000 copies. This was a very shrewd marketing move for two reasons. Firstly by issuing such a limited edition it generated a heavy demand for the single in its first week on sale as Ash fans raced to the shops to secure their copy, thereby almost guaranteeing a chart placing – the single crashed into the charts at number 38, a real achievement for a band that had barely been going for six months in any professional sense. The second advantage of the collector's single is that it creates a buzz about a band, makes the release of a single a real event. It also commits your following to the band, gives them something extra to look forward and increases their devotion. In the early days, it is crucial that you develop a hard-core audience as soon as possible, for it is from that fan base that a larger audience can be constructed. They are, in effect, the advance guard for your band, telling friends at school, college or work about this great new band whose stuff they collect religiously. For Ash, that advance guard made a huge difference to their chances of success, and they mobilised it with an almost military precision.

Likewise they did not underestimate the value of radio exposure either. Taking full advantage of their spell in England, they recorded a second BBC session for the *Evening Session*, performing 'Jack Names The Planets', 'American Devil', 'Coasting' and 'Girl From Mars', the latter providing further evidence of their increasing confidence and songwriting ability. But these days were really all about the Elastica tour and the uniformly ecstatic response they elicited. Playing at the Irish Centre in Leeds, the *NME*'s Lisa Hoftijzer was in attendance to witness the final emergence of the next great rock band, playing with all the exuberance one would expect: 'Tim and Mark thrash out, wreaking apparent havoc while putting all the right noises in all the right places before their mother comes home. David Gedge is to be found wandering around in the background like a proud parent ... Ash have special dispensation to skip school on this Elastica support tour and, like true yoof rebels, they have neglected to do the homework set them on the road, so they may have some catching up to do back at college. When it comes to the simple pleasures of joyful music though, it's the others who lag behind.' Later in the year, when tipping Ash as the band to watch in 1995, *Melody Maker* pointed out, 'Anyone who turned up early at Elastica's October shows was left scraping their jaw off the floor after the incendiary antics of show openers Ash. Their brief set was the high point of a year which saw them explode from their native Northern Ireland with a trio of gloriously noisy, unashamedly pop singles.'

On stage, with just a thirty-minute slot to fill, Ash were allowed to go all-out with no need to pace their set. They came on, plugged in and thrashed away for half an hour, making an impact that few support bands could equal. Being a support act can be a thankless business – the audience is, after all, there to see somebody else and rock fans are not renowned for their infinite reserves of patience. On the other hand, if you approach it with the right attitude, as Ash did, supporting a band like Elastica can be the passport to success. It was clear from the very outset that Ash would make the most of this opportunity and they were soon carried along by the sheer pace of events.

Off stage too, the tour was an education and a lot of fun. Elastica were not miffed by Ash's success since they were adding to the shows, not detracting attention away from the main act. Tim said, 'They were really cool. We beat them up in a street fight in Wolverhampton. Mark threw Justine over his shoulder!' The entire tour was great fun and was their introduction to real touring, the 'proper insanity' as Mark had termed it. Although they had been no slouches when it came to drinking in the past, being on the road gave them the excuse and the freedom to embrace hedonism with real enthusiasm.

It is no surprise that rock bands have such lusty appetites for good times night after night. Look at their basic, average day. Get up in a strange hotel, eat, sit in a hotel lobby with nothing to do, get on a bus, travel a hundred miles or more while reading, watching a video, listening to some music or sleeping. Arrive at another hotel, check in, sit around waiting to go to the venue. Get there, soundcheck, eat, sit around waiting for show time. Rock'n'roll might look glamorous but basically it is a lot of hanging around, punctuated by a comparatively brief burst of excitement on stage, the tedium often lightened by a bottle. Having been bored all day, a band has to crank itself up to fever pitch for their performance and then comes on with adrenalin raging through their collective system and wondering what to do. Sleep is inevitably elusive due to the residual excitement and the fact that they might have already slept on the bus earlier in the day. What are you to do but find a club and have a drink or six to unwind, particularly as your fans are only too ready to buy them for you? And once you are in a club and you are equipped with some spending money, there is every chance that you might use the alcohol to wash down the odd pharmaceutical, which as we all know, are only too readily available. And if it was there to be had, Ash had it. In spades. Steven Wells best summed up the relish with which they attacked the dissolute lifestyle in *Vox* a year later when he wrote a feature piece on their behaviour on tour, pointing out that

Kung Fu's for kids. We want water pistols – Rick, Tim, Mark.

Wanted – all the trappings of rock 'n' roll success

(below)
Real pop stars, November 1995.

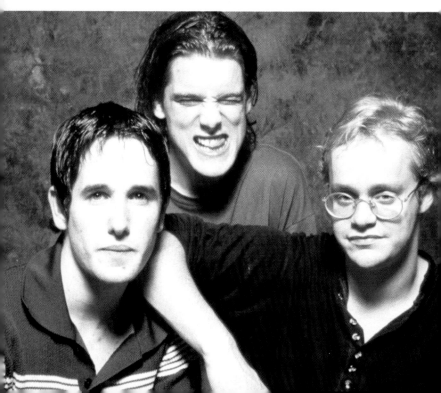

In desperate need of a makeover

Just
good
friends

London Forum, 24 May 1996.
Tim Wheeler (above)
and Mark Hamilton (right)

Tim Wheeler: rock 'n' roll animal

Knee-deep in grass, July 1996.

(left) Tim at the Brits, February 1997.

(below) World-weary travellers, Irving Plaza, New York, July 1996.

Mark is suddenly possessed, New York, July 1996.

for them, this was the first time around the block. 'You're thinking "how childish, how puerile, how dated, clichéd, passé, boring". And this will be because, like me, you're too old. Yes, rock piggery is creakingly clichéd behaviour. Yes it's been done before – but like oral sex and frenzied guitar wanking, if it is done with vim and vigour, it is always a crowd pleaser . . . who the fuck wants sensible rock bands? We want and need a thousand acne encrusted Antichrists drinking and drugging and transit vanning themselves to death for our sins.'

As Mark pointed out, 'The lifestyle's there and it is free every night. Students, other people our age do this as often as they can. We can just get away with it more. I was born to it, getting hammered and playing songs. You're on a massive high when you come off stage and it'd be bad to stop it. It's just normal teenage behaviour.' Mark's rationalisation of Ash's antics was fair comment, though it belied the fact that it could easily get out of hand, to the detriment of their health. It was probably just as well that, during this period, touring was limited to short, sharp shocks as they became accustomed to it. Even so, that did not stop them playing their first European dates when they supported the dismal Dodgy and the wonderful Salad at the Amsterdam Paradiso in November 1994. The *NME*'s John Harris filed the traditionally enthusiastic review, adding a couple of important caveats to his praise: 'Brilliantly young, like people suspended on elastic bands, they have reverentially hurled every member of the common room aristocracy (Weddoes, Pixies, Neds) into an adolescent furnace. The result is frequently drabsville, only it is shot with enough incendiary exceptions to suggest that an attitude transfusion, a uniform that aims higher than Milletts and two years of hard knocks might just turn them into something remarkable.'

Harris's point about their consigning The Wedding Present et al to history was valid and made it perfectly clear just how fast the turnover in the indie sector was, such that it was almost keeping pace with that of the pop charts. In days of yore, an indie band would get at least half a dozen years at the top but now the sixth-formers were rejecting anything that their elder brothers or sisters might have played and were embracing new acts such as Elastica, Blur and Ash with almost evangelical zeal. While that acted to Ash's advantage at this stage, it was a development to which they had to pay attention if they did not want to go the same way as those bands five years down the line. Ash needed to broaden both their songwriting and their overall appeal.

With their touring duties over for the moment, they returned to the wacky world of further education to continue with their studies. For Mark, this was almost more than he could bear. In a lot of ways, Mark was the most committed to the idea of an alternative lifestyle, an escape from convention. It was he, after all, who had helped organise the *Raptor Presents* sampler in an attempt to gain wider recognition for Ash. Having now gone out on the road, tasted the acclaim of the fans, had some minor chart success and glimpsed the possibilities that lay in front of them, he wanted more, he wanted it all and he wanted it now. Having been allowed to drop his economic studies, he turned his attention to hanging around the art room all day, longing for the call to get back out on the road. 'I hated going back to school. It just didn't make any sense to me. We'd be coming over here [to the mainland] on tours and having the best time ever, and then we'd get back to school and be treated like shit. Like we were little kids or something. I suppose I had a bad attitude,' said Mark.

Where Tim could treat the whole thing as a diversion, and a funny one at that – 'When you can't hand in some work, the teachers tend not to have heard "Sorry, sir, but I was supporting Elastica last night" as an excuse!' – for Mark it was more serious than that. If anything, that situation was about to get worse since from out of a clear blue sky, Pearl Jam's Eddie Vedder put in a personal call to their London management to see if Ash would care to support Pearl Jam on the south-east Asian leg of their world tour. This was a real chance to see the world, watch one of the world's biggest bands at close hand, achieve more exposure in a few weeks than you could in months of slogging around the dives they'd been playing, and make a bag of money into the bargain. For any putative rocker, this was too good to be true. But it conflicted with school exams and the band turned it down, Tim saying, 'It would have been a good experience to tour with such a big band but we don't actually like them that much.' In fact, turning down Pearl Jam, and in such a cool, offhand, dismissive fashion, was the best thing they could have done. It won them scores of column inches and marked them out as a band to be reckoned with. How could a batch of seventeen-year-olds be so arrogant as to kick Eddie Vedder into touch – they must be worth a look. As a piece of elegant PR, it ranked with the very best, but in the short term Mark must have been disappointed.

Fortunately, there was something to take his mind off things, the late October release of *Trailer*, a mini album which collected together the best bits of their material to date, one which had been recorded over the course of the summer holidays from school. Essentially a clearing the decks operation to leave them free to concentrate on their first album proper once school finished for good the following summer, *Trailer* was an eclectic, though patchy collection of songs. It is not surprising that the best material was made up of the three singles, 'Jack Names The Planets', 'Petrol' and 'Uncle Pat', Although the remaining songs were just as worthy of the attention, if only as an indication of where Ash had come from and where they might go.

Some of the songs were less than perfect – in truth some had barely a nodding acquaintance with that ideal. The grungy noise-metal floundering of 'Obscure Thing' – described by *NME*'s Ian Watson as 'combining a metallic teeth grinding stomp while chanting a love letter to Satan', was pretty dreadful, an exercise in macho music making that would have been better suited to a Napalm Death album than an Ash collection. 'Get Out' was the obvious result of too great a flirtation with The Wedding Present canon, the result sounding like anything that they or The

Wonder Stuff might have released. Snotty, noisy, enjoyable, it did not add anything desperately new to the sum of human knowledge and had 'filler' written all over it. Some suggested that these failings could be attributed to their tender age but this was so much rubbish. These were not the failings of youth per se, but those of musical inexperience. Ash were still not a full-time band. To say they had been together for two years or more was a little misleading. The actual time they had spent together, actually *being* Ash, was far shorter, and of course it takes time for a band to really come together properly; in that regard, Mark's desire for them to get together was rooted in solid good sense.

You not only need to learn how to be a band, you also have to learn how to be a songwriter, and how to write songs that play to the strengths of your group. It may be an art form, but it is also a craft. The seven songs that *Trailer* showcased were among the very first that had tumbled from Ash's collective pens and so it was scarcely surprising that they were a pretty mixed bag. As with any art form, songwriting takes plenty of practice, a lot of intense work and concentration before you can really get it right. There might be a naive charm to your earliest efforts – that much was true of something like 'Uncle Pat' – but they are seldom sturdy enough to stand the test of time.

Songwriting is much more to do with applying skills rather than simply accumulating them. What marks out the great songwriters is their ability to channel these techniques in such a way that their instinctive, natural talents can be unleashed, expressed to the fullest. The truly great song-writers are 90% perspiration, 10% inspiration, but it is that 10% of genius that is the crucial element. These are the musical equivalent of an Eric Cantona, a Brian Lara, a Tiger Woods. For the rest, the average musicians who clog up the airwaves, the journeymen for whom perspiration is 99% of the equation, these are your basic Vinnie Jones model. *Trailer* represented Ash's stint in the reserves prior to the step up to the full side. There were enough glimpses of genius with songs like 'Jack Names The Planets' to suggest that they would thrive in the rarefied atmosphere of the first team, but enough faults such as 'Obscure Thing' to indicate that further hard work was required.

Nevertheless, this offering was welcomed with open arms by *Hot Press*, Liam Fay arguing, 'It proves conclusively that by any standards, Ash are a rock band of genuine stature. Their age is irrelevant, a matter between them and their local off-licence.' *NME*'s Emma Morgan agreed, awarding the album seven marks out of ten. She said 'Youth is cool and crinkly rock is shit. Ash, pop-pubescents to a lad, should be the coolest band in the world bar none . . . it seems that, if they get those awful haircuts sorted out sharpish, they could have a chance of being our best weapon against the dinosaurs,' though there was a hint of them being damned with faint praise. Liam Fay's review was altogether more enthusiastic, extolling the virtues of their 'bone dry sense of humour and their eye for un-nervingly absurd detail . . . [a] warped and toxic undertow . . . teeth gnashing guitars, pile driving drums, melancholy, eerie vocals . . . [Trailer] packs a ballistic punch but is also instantly alluring . . . [these] trash virtuosos have mastered one of rock's greatest tricks, the art of bullet-headed charm.' With praise such as that, it was little wonder that Ash were twice nominated in the Smithwicks-sponsored *Hot Press* awards for 1994, lining themselves up for the Best Irish single award for 'Petrol' and the Philip Lynott award for best new band – a genuine thrill given their fondness for Thin Lizzy.

Not all was praise however. Returning to Emma Morgan's review, she made mention of 'the detectable themes of Nirvana chords, Gedge voice and Nedsesque melodies on at least half of the songs. This is not necessarily bad although it could become a little dull over the course of a full album perhaps (hint hint). Here it is endearing, just don't push it.' Morgan was quite right to suggest that a little more diversity would be a good thing, but equally astute was Leo Finlay in his *Vox* review of the album: 'Ash's greatest strength lies in direct blasts of power pop.' Even at this early stage, it was obvious that Ash were at their most successful, most attractive, most emotionally affecting when they kept it simple and let the songs soar as with 'Petrol'. Great pop writers do not come around so regularly that we can afford to let them waste their talents and it was strikingly obvious that Tim Wheeler was a great pop writer in the making. With *Trailer*, it was clear that he was torn between the lo-fi grunge of 'Intense Thing' and the sublime pop of 'Jack Names The Planets'. It is certainly not unusual for a band to follow such diverse themes -The Cure have been doing it for years – but in these days when singles are more important than they have ever been, would Ash follow the sensible path of crafting a bunch of pop classics in order to win over an audience before unleashing their other tastes on the world?

5.

ONE SICK PARTY

You might well call 1994 a pretty remarkable year for Ash. Having started the year as virtual nobodies, still searching for a post-school career, they ended it touted as 'the next big thing'. They'd put out three highly acclaimed singles, signed to one of the more influential of the independent labels, released a mini-album that had both underlined their potential and left the way clear for them to find a viable future direction, toured with bands like Elastica, Ride and Babes In Toyland, told Eddie Vedder just where he could stick his Pearl Jam, and built a reputation as one of the best live bands on the UK circuit. Not bad for a year's work. As Tim self-deprecatingly noted, 'It's harder being rock'n'roll when you're a whippersnapper, but it's more fun trying.'

But if 1994 had been good, 1995 promised to be a whole lot better. Six months of school to go and then they would be free to become Ash full-time. Picking up their passport to debauchery on the way, they could become the full-on rock'n'roll band of their dreams. Certainly the year dawned in auspicious fashion with the arrival of a brand new song, 'Kung Fu'. If that was not enough, America was suddenly calling out their name with a couple of very major labels desperate for their signature. Did life get any better than this?

Maybe there is some cosmic karmic force, maybe in deference to such *Star Wars* lovers, The Force, which decrees there has to be some overall balance in life. For just as everything was going right, just as suddenly, it all went wrong. Mark had been giving cause for concern for a little while now, his obvious frustration with being stuck in school eating away at him. Candidly, he admitted, 'I loathed it, I didn't want to be there, the pressure of everything really got to me and I just got really sick.' Such a matter of fact statement does not tell half of the story, a story which threatened not only the future of the band, but that of Mark himself.

None but those who have been there can fully appreciate the strain that Mark was under. Where Tim was a more phlegmatic character, equably taking all the events in his stride, Mark let everything that was going on get under his skin. The Ash lifestyle was a pretty kinetic one, a perplexing mish-mash of mundanity and madness. If school helped Tim and Rick retain a sense of balance, it threw Mark off kilter. Already frustrated by simply being in school rather than pillaging his way across south-east Asia in Pearl Jam's wake, not only did he have to deal with the misery of being there, he was fretting over taking his art exams the following summer. Having missed so much school and been so disenchanted with it when he was there, he was lacking in confidence. Anyone who's had to cram desperately before exams knows exactly what he was going through. What we mere mortals do not have is the added pressure of having to make international deals which are potentially worth millions of dollars at the same time. As Ash became increasingly successful and as the American companies got ready to swoop down up them, Mark could be forgiven for thinking that he was carrying the weight of the music industry on his shoulders. Into that volatile equation has to be added the real X-factor. Mark's sense of perspective, never his greatest quality, was further distorted by his enthusiastic intake of a variety of drink and drugs, much of which came free. It did not help that he was suddenly making a very decent living and, since he was still living at home, had little else to spend his money on but himself. He said, 'Being in the band has given me an opportunity to spend even more money on *Star Wars* stuff than ever before. I'd never spend all my cash on it, but it is a pretty high percentage, like 97%!' Even were that true, the rest surely went on recreational refreshment.

Entering the confessional in the course of a *Hot Press* interview, it was alleged that Mark had taken a tab of acid and had then taken a full three months to come down from its effects. This is certainly plausible, the more so since he has made no secret of his liking for pharmaceuticals. In addition, as a public face, he would be the recipient of free drugs in clubs the length and breadth of the country. In that situation, you can have no idea of the quality or potency of what you are taking. Equally, it might be that some bright spark might have thought it amusing to try out a particularly venomous dose of acid on the famous pop star. It was a possibility he denied, insisting that drugs were not the cause. Whatever the root of the problem, the effects were terrifying. As he told *Select*, 'I was in an unbelievably bad way when I was sick. When you freak out on acid and everything becomes like hell, well that is what I was like for six months. And I hadn't even taken anything. I was just so tense about school, family, drugs, everything. But when my family saw me strapped into the hospital bed and they saw what a vulnerable situation I was in, they rallied around. There was love there that never seemed to be before. It was a positive outcome.'

Certainly stress can take a savage toll on the human mind, and it is perfectly possible that Mark's illness was purely psychological, his mind simply shutting down as the only sane response to what he was going through. However, in *Melody Maker,* he covered his tracks and told a slightly different story: 'I had some sort of breakdown. Too many drugs. It was mid-February and I couldn't do anything. It was a Sunday night when it all started. It was like an acid freak-out but instead of going away, it stayed. I just couldn't get my head round anything at all. I was properly messed up. I couldn't watch TV for any more than seven seconds. I couldn't write anything. I couldn't concentrate on anything. It scared the shit out of me. I used to be a devious wee bastard. I'd do anything to get my own way, but I'm better now [after being so sick]. I used to be mad for everything. It was good getting off my head and then being normal the next day. But getting off my head and then staying off my head, that wasn't so good. I just wanted to be normal, I didn't want to be dead.' *Melody Maker* hammered home the point of Mark's irresponsibility by printing a litany of drugs that he had allegedly sampled when revelling in the band's early success, basking in the light of that vital recording contract. The list included LSD, E, whizz, dope and even, on just one occasion, heroin. It seems that the 'Just Say No' campaign had rather passed Mark by.

Mark was in such a bad way that he went through a veritable hospital's worth of psychologists but to no avail. He said, 'I was just this total paranoid wreck. I was seeing shrinks all the time but they all just fuck me up even more. I had a spell when I was in hospital when I thought the whole world was one big conspiracy, that everyone knew something I didn't. I used to get in desperate states.' Gradually he began to come out of the dark tunnel, with the crucial role in his rehabilitation being played by family and friends if his song 'I Need Somebody' is anything to go by. This track, the b-side of 'Goldfinger', as described by *Melody Maker*'s Ben Stud, is 'a weird, funny and genuinely alarming tale of drug abuse and its consequence'. According to Stud, Mark penned the song when he was lying in hospital thinking about how and why he wasn't dead.

If the illness was a harrowing experience for Mark, it was no bundle of laughs for Rick and Tim either. Mark was struck down just a matter of days before they were set to fly out to Los Angeles to be wined and dined by the American recording industry, with Warner Brothers and Interscope laying on the very best in entertainment in order to impress them. Bribery and corruption? No such thing. Whatever the case, it was obvious that Mark could not go, though everyone played down the severity of his illness – after all, no one wanted to let the company that would be bankrolling their future know that there might not be any future. For Tim, 'Mark's illness provided four days of total fear. I thought if I could just grin and bear it, it would go away. But it didn't. It just got worse. The worst came when we heard he was having brain scans.' Those brain scans provided no clue as to the causes of Mark's illness, so ultimately it became a case of healing himself. Perhaps the support of his family was the key, perhaps it was simply the fact that he stepped off the treadmill for a while, albeit in dramatic fashion. Maybe the effect of the drugs wore off if they had been the cause; or perhaps the shock of this near-death experience was enough to give him a life-saving shot of perspective. Whatever the case, Mark, thankfully, began to recover as his band mates were busily sealing their material future in far off California.

In mid-February, Tim and Rick left a shivering Downpatrick and flew into California to be greeted by temperatures of 95 degrees. Lounging in one of Los Angeles' finer hotels, they had their pick of pool, sauna, drink, food, or whatever else they wanted, and the opportunity to stick it all on someone else's tab, all of which would have been unbelievable a few short months before. Now, corporate America was falling over itself to get its hands on Ash. Just as fate had given them a helping hand with the arrival of Therapy?, which had put the spotlight on Northern Ireland, and then with the launch of the New Wave of New Wave which added to the attention lavished on them, Ash were now lucky that the wheel of musical fashion in the States was turning their way. After the grit and grime of Nirvana had reintroduced the concept of punk rock to the American charts, a more malleable version was being sought. The same had happened back in the mid-1980s when a more palatable kind of heavy metal was discovered, bringing multiple millions of sales to Def Leppard and Bon Jovi, the pioneers of metal lite. Now Green Day had outstripped Nirvana's success and with similarly-minded artists like Soul Asylum and Offspring doing equally well, diet punk was all the rage.

The similarities between Green Day and Ash are so obvious as to need no further explanation – the same attitude, the same sound, the same poppy roots, the same sort of attack. Given America's anglophile tastes however, the chances were that Ash could eclipse even their success, having both musical and novelty value, their youth doing them no harm either. Ultimately, the choice of an American label boiled down to Interscope or Warner Brothers. Warners were already the home of Green Day and so they were clearly one step ahead of the competition but Interscope's attentions were equally flattering. Not only were they flattering, they were great fun too. The *NME*'s

Keith Cameron accompanied Rick and Tim on their American jaunt and filed a report filled with ever more descriptive accounts of Rick's penchant for getting remarkably drunk incredibly quickly followed by the inevitable flushing out of his stomach – the headline 'Boys Who Like Hurls' was a pretty accurate description. If only Mark had been there, he could have passed on his hangover cure-all, though in truth, it is not advisable to follow his prescription: 'The best cure I've developed is a chemical cocktail consisting of grass, beta blockers and valium washed down by as much water as you can drink without peeing.' On the whole, you are probably better off with just the hangover.

Tim admitted that this kind of life could go to your head: 'You get used to the idea of record companies fawning over you and I suppose you start to expect it. Which is pretty bad!' If the American trip proved anything, it was the change in Rick, previously nicknamed 'Rock' by the rest of the band for his non-rock'n'roll, geek-like tendencies. As Tim explained, 'He was the quiet one at the start and now he's the hard-core one!' Mark was a little more colourful in his description: 'From geek to wild, dress wearing, bleached haired, fag-smoking, no-shame, willing to be humiliated, rock'n'roll animal.' Putting away sufficient drink to last him a lifetime in the unlikely event of the return of prohibition, Rick was fast catching up with Mark's in the wanton hedonism stakes – given that Mark was currently laid up in hospital, the wisdom of such action has to be questioned. Still, kids eh?

Interscope's chances took a real dip while they were
wining and dining our heroes, taking them to Johnny
Depp's club, The Viper Room. Watching a dismal band on
stage, dead ringers for Huey Lewis And The News,
Interscope's representatives let slip that they might be
signing them! Even in spite of this dreadful lapse in taste,
Tim saw only the good side of the American industry,
reminding us again of the band's desire and determination
to succeed all around the globe. 'The industry is a lot more
down to earth than you'd expect. We met a few flash "rock
biz" types but really everyone's just trying to do their job as
honestly and efficiently as they can. There was no bullshit
from the A&R people we were dealing with and my advice
to bands who don't like Americans or the way they do
business is "stay at home". Radio One during the daytime
just play teenybop trash which only sells on image. In
America, alternative music is the mainstream now. It makes
you realise that you don't have to spend your life going
round the small indie circuit,' said Tim. As far as America
was concerned, there seemed just one drawback for him.
'We were in a restaurant and I was about to order a beer
and the waiter said, "How old are you?" Then he said, "I
can get you a root beer." It was quite humiliating.'

Again, Ash demonstrated that they were from a whole
different era and with a totally different approach to the
indie bands that had gone before. The likes of Echo & The
Bunnymen, The Wonder Stuff, The Cure or The Mission
could never have made such a statement and got away with
it. For any band in the 1980s, the orthodoxy was to avoid

talk of money and success at all times and pretend that you were happy to stay in your ghetto – that your art was all. For Ash, children of the Thatcherite years, there was no longer any need to be embarrassed by making pots of money. If you did not make money, you were not doing it right. Ash had already jumped on that particular bandwagon when Heineken had provided them with a healthy wad for their participation in an Irish beer commercial, 'Uncle Pat' providing the soundtrack. Five years earlier, that would have been unforgivable, prompting cries of sell-out, but Ash were a whole lot more relaxed over the whole affair. Tim's view was simple: 'I'd love to be able to say that we had a really long and heated debate about whether it would affect our artistic credibility, but really we just wanted to know how much money they were going to give us! Most bands wait until they are successful before selling out. We've done it straight away. We rather naively thought we'd get away with it, but unbeknown to us the director decided to include a close-up of the *Trailer* CD box which blew our cover! Seriously though, having that thirty seconds of "Uncle Pat" included in the commercial will do more for us profile wise in Ireland than doing a dozen *Late Late* shows [Ireland's most popular entertainment show]. Actually, we've got a nice, tasteful instrumental break which we're going to send to all the tampon companies!'

On their return from the States, Ash had to make their final decision on a US company. In the end, they came down on the side of Warners for a five-album deal, signing to their

Reprise label. According to Tim, 'We told Reprise that we wanted money to make a Manga cartoon film starring us and they agreed. It'll be a sci-fi comic strip action movie. Everyone will have super powers and the plot is that we're on tour in Japan and we have to save the world. It'll be brilliant.' The Japanese reference unwittingly made it obvious just how important getting a deal in America had been. Once they had Warners on their side, the whole world was about to open up for them. There was no territory that was beyond them. Ash were really on the way.

Thankfully, not only had they signed a great deal, but Mark was on his way back to something approaching full health. Glancing at the 108-page contract for their American adventure, he tossed it aside, saying 'I can't be bothered to read it.' Nevertheless, he was as thrilled as the other two to find that their future was pretty much assured, something which may have played a part in his on-going recovery, lifting at least one of the weights from his shoulders. A slot on the Glastonbury bill was confirmation that Ash were a big name in their home territory, though it still did not prepare them for the attention that surrounded the release of their next single, 'Kung Fu', in March. Even though this one only reached number fifty-seven in the charts, something of a drop after the success of 'Uncle Pat', it was 'Kung Fu' which really established them in the hearts and minds of indie-pop followers everywhere. Such was the impression it made, it picked up the 'Single of the Week' award in *NME* and was finally voted in at number thirty-three in their 'Singles of the Year' poll at the end of the year.

The *NME* reaction was ecstatic, bordering on the religious: 'Packs in every cliché there's ever been about the exotic east and sounds dumb beyond measure. In short, this is a blinder, a celebratory youthquake. Do not despise the carefree teenager. If you do, you know nish all about the human condition, grasshopper.' Michael Bonner's praise in *Melody Maker* was tinged with cynicism and a prediction he doubtless regrets: 'Ash are fearsome whirlwinds of noisy reckless teenage energy and this ferocious little sidewinder is their best vinyl outing yet. Sadly, as they don't live within vomiting distance of the Westway [obviously he hadn't seen just how far they could vomit] and don't have famous girlfriends, they will never be the stars they should which is a terrible triumph for style over substance.'

Ash's Ramones tribute – the teenage lobotomy reference was a dead giveaway – it was also their homage to the world of martial arts movies. The sound of 1977, this was just a wonderful slab of adrenalin-pop, mindless melody, inane lyrics, the ideal soundtrack to a drunken party or for filling the dance-floor on indie night. Tim admitted, 'I came up with it after I'd been listening non-stop to The Ramones for a couple of days over Christmas. It is more inspiration than actual stealing though. At the same time I fell in love with the words "Kung Fu", "Hong Kong" and "Fu Manchu". We wanted to write a really crap Ramones song and we only thought it was going to be a B-side. It was a fluke. Written in five minutes, recorded less than a day later in two minutes, fifteen seconds. Adding anything else would have ruined it. It's only later, when I was a wee bit

distanced from it, that I realised it's a pretty cool song.'
Even the sleeve featured some cunning pillaging of popular
culture – with Manchester United's Eric Cantona now the
nation's leading exponent of the drop-kick following his
attack on a member of the crowd at Selhurst Park in
January 1995, he became the ideal cover star and featured
prominently on the 'Japanese' artwork used on the
wraparound sleeve of the limited edition seven-inch.

The band's fascination with pop culture spilled over
into the b-sides too. 'Day Of The Triffids' dropped names
like Dr. No, Fu Manchu (again), the Hooded Claw and
Hannibal Lechter, while 'Luther Ingo's Star Cruiser' was
simply a more subtle name for 'I Wanna Fuck You Up The
Ass', a title which Tim's father had forbade him to use on
pain of refusing to allow him to sign his publishing
contract. The senior Wheeler had it right for if there is one
aspect of their age that did act against Ash, it was their
inevitable delight in the scatological and their propensity to
let boozy in-jokes make it on to record. What sounds funny
on a Friday night after eight pints of lager and a curry is not
always side-splitting when committed to vinyl and played
back for the umpteenth time. 'Luther Ingo's Star Cruiser'
might just be a song that will come back to haunt them in
ten years.

Minor quibbles such as this aside, 'Kung Fu' was yet
another example of the speed with which Ash were
improving. There was a brief flying visit to England for a
few dates through the Easter holidays in support of 'Kung
Fu', though a bit late in the day to boost its chart rating and

then it was heads down for the final stretch towards the exams. After that, surely nothing could stand between Ash and world domination?

6.

SCHOOL'S OUT.
COMPLETELY

Remember that last day of school? Great wasn't it, the overwhelming feeling of relief. It is not always like that, not like that for everyone. Where Ash were concerned, it was all rather different. Rick had already left of course, and was living in limbo at university. Mark's academic career had pretty well folded and he failed to turn up for his exams, though his course work was good enough to guarantee him a grade B pass in Art. Tim, meanwhile, had to slog his way through his three final papers, though he emerged to say 'I'm glad I took them, it made my parents very happy.' The final moment was a real anti-climax. 'I did my Maths A-level and then went out for a meal with my friends. Then the next day we went off to play at Glastonbury. I didn't feel anything,' said Tim. It is fair to say that playing at Glastonbury knocks spots off signing on the dole after you have finished your finals, so it is no surprise that Tim was distinctly underwhelmed by this particular rite of passage. Equally, there was no big plan on which to focus on how to get out of Northern Ireland. Tim pointed out, 'You only have to move to London to get a record deal which we didn't have to do. It's a weird place Northern Ireland. No one seems to have any great ambition there. It seems so foreign, but I know I belong to it. I'll always love my wee house by the river.'

Glastonbury is one of the more remarkable features of the English summer, a festival that gathers together enormous numbers of people to see a genuinely eclectic mix of artists, artists who you would never see together anywhere else but in the middle of the West Country. For Ash, it was their biggest gig to date, no question, and it went off surprisingly well. In her summation of the event, *Select*'s Gina Morris gave them seven out of ten, marks Tim would have gladly taken for his A-levels. Morris went on to remark on their 'witty but dumb lyrics, pop magnetism and Black Sabbathesque guitar', pointing out that 'they all looked so nervous and overawed you could almost see them shaking'. However, they were not so overawed by their fame that they did not have the good sense to turn down the chance to support Soul Asylum in Europe.

The whole idea of fame, being in the papers, seeing the right faces, was something that did not much appeal to the band at this stage. Tim said then, 'Some bands live for having their names in the press. But if I'd got shit-faced and started a fight in a club, then I'd want to keep it quiet, but there are people who actually feed that to the journalists because they know it's worth a couple of column inches. We've never got involved with that nonsense which is partly because we don't want to, and partly because we've all been studying for our A-levels when the decent parties have been on!' That puritanical streak did not last too much longer, but even back then it highlighted a conflict in the band, Mark explaining, 'I don't care how people see us. But I know Tim does, big style. He's got more to say. I'm just having fun.'

There again, even Tim could get a bit miffed about their low profile. They were an internationally signed band after all, but back in Downpatrick, the locals were not too impressed: 'A lot of people round here wouldn't have realised what we were doing because to start with we played at weekends and then later, we stopped playing here. People here are ignorant of what's happening. Since I got my exam results, they keep saying, "So, you're going to university next year then?" Which is mildly insulting!' By July, Tim was the proud possessor of three A-level qualifications, two grade Bs and a C. He was the equally proud possessor of a huge hit single.

Their finest release to that date, the delightful, wistful, whimsy of 'Girl From Mars' had crashed into the UK charts at number eleven, kicking up a storm. Startlingly bright, if it had any ancestors, they would have been The Cure's 'Catch' or 'Just Like Heaven', shafts of incandescent pop sunlight that finally, irrevocably and irrefutably dismissed any lingering doubts about Ash's popcore credentials. Its acoustic start, its Lizzyesque guitar break, the Pete Shelley vocals and infusion of attitude made it the perfect summer single. Ultimately, if Ash go on to true greatness, the roots of that greatness will be traced back to the day 'Girl From

Mars' was released. As the *NME*'s Ian Watson noted, 'It smiles sweetly while applying a hobnail to your guts.' Rick's description was a little more graceful, after he had made the obligatory joke about it being written for Marianne Faithfull: 'It's to do with summer exuberance and being young.'

The demands put on any up and coming band can be extreme at the best of the times, but those placed on Ash were unforgivably so. They had already cost Mark his health – contributing, at least in part, to his breakdown – and they now conspired to rob them of some of the best moments of immediate post-adolescence – good exam results and release from school. On top of that, they did not even have the time really to reflect on what 'Girl From Mars' had achieved, for they were never off the treadmill – summer was one manic whirl of gigs. In addition, they repaid their debt to Mark Radcliffe for his championing of 'Jack Names The Planets' with a session for his Radio One show, blasting out 'Kung Fu', 'Girl From Mars', 'Uncle Pat' and 'Punk Boy'. As Tim ruefully commented, 'We were so busy this summer there was no time to get excited. Every so often, I'd have a minute to sit back and think, "Yeah, number eleven; I can look back in twenty years and be proud." But the charts haven't meant much for the last few years anyway . . . it's like that bit in *Star Wars* where Darth Vader says, "The force is strong within you but you're not a Jedi yet." That's what we used to be but now we are Jedis. And we will be Jedi masters when our album comes out.'

If this new single had brought Ash to wider attention, it was on the live circuit that they were now making their reputation, playing venues booked well before 'Girl From Mars' had made its impact. Consequently, they and their ever expanding audience were shoehorned into tiny clubs that were far too small; places like Manchester's Boardwalk could have been filled three times over. However, this enforced closeness meant that the gigs reached hysterical proportions – Ash were to the summer of 1995 what The Stone Roses had been to the spring of 1989, a band that was breaking big all over the country while they were actually on the road, the momentum that they were creating threatening to swamp them. Happily, unlike the Roses, Ash were not churlish enough to blow dates out in the knowledge they could return to a bigger venue a month or so later. Instead, they just enjoyed the 'School's Out Forever' tour.

So did the fans if the *NME* review of their gig at the Bristol Fleece is any guide at all: 'An event with absolutely no agenda at all and where everything you learned about pop music in the gilded palace of cliché has come true. When Tim says he hasn't slept for three days, there are screams of approval because this sounds appreciably different from what someone eighteen years old should be doing. It sounds glamorous instead. [Nevertheless the] fearsomely heavy Nirvana grinds that leave their bubble-gum years momentarily behind point towards them getting aggressively older.' In fact, those 'Nirvana moments' were misleading, for if anything Ash were moving away from that school of songwriting and towards a sharper pop focus. On stage, most songs were played faster and louder, the natural atmosphere of real excitement created at the gig seeing to that, but it was becoming increasingly plain that Ash were at their very best when they kept the idea of tunes and melodies uppermost in their minds.

With that goal in mind, their recruitment of Owen Morris as producer had been a masterstroke. The producer behind Oasis's success, his work on 'Girl From Mars' and 'Kung Fu' before that made it clear that he and Ash made a perfect combination. Morris had a highly developed ear for great British pop in the best traditions of The Kinks, The Beatles and The Who, never sacrificing power for commercialism, but neither did he confuse volume for intensity, a failing that Ash had been guilty of in the past on *Trailer*. As an arranger and as someone who can readily identify a song's strengths, he is without peer at present. His skill is to ensure that each track is presented in its most sympathetic guise, free of unnecessary clutter. If a song can be played on acoustic guitar, fine; if it needs heavy guitars and distortion, so be it. Certainly the arrival of Morris coincided with the release of better and better Ash material; but before all the credit goes to him, remember that a producer, however good, can only work with the material he is given. There is no doubt that as songwriters, Ash were going through an exponential improvement.

Morris's reputation was already secure when he and Ash first got together and clearly his arrival gave the band extra confidence in themselves. Even so, his working practices were a little odd, to say the least. Ash were still very inexperienced in the highly unnatural studio environment, and it was Morris's job to relax them, so such pranks as were played did much to lighten the atmosphere. Rick – it had to be Rick, butt of all jokes – was forced to wear a dress. 'And it was a crap dress too. Strapless. Quite glittery though,' he added, seemingly warming to the idea. Yet more welcome were Morris's drinking habits which dovetailed perfectly with Ash's own views on the subject. According to Tim, 'Every time, we'll have been recording for a couple of hours and he'll suddenly say, "Right, down the pub for a swift half." And we end up staying in the pub for about two hours getting pissed. The more you work at it, it gets quicker. We normally end up pushed for time because we're in the pub so much!'

Morris was of course a bit pushed for time himself, being one of the most in-demand producers in the country. As a result, he could not hang around while Ash put the finishing touches to the b-sides for 'Girl From Mars', 'Cantina Band' and 'Astral Conversations With Toulouse-Lautrec'. For Rick, b-sides offered a welcome chance to experiment. 'I wouldn't say it was throwaway, just very spontaneous. Most of our b-sides are very strange. I'm not really sure where they're going!' This time, Phil Thornalley formerly with The Cure, circa 'The Top', was drafted in for a production alliance that was not to run smoothly. Tim recalls, 'We didn't get on, so to fuck him off we took what was basically two riffs and jammed around them. It was a one-take special that should have sounded terrible but actually turned out brilliantly.' 'Cantina Band' was yet another nod in the direction of *Star Wars*, grisly bar music from the film. By now, Mark, the number one devotee in the ranks, had seen the three *Star Wars* epics 'in all honesty, more than 200 times each'.

By now, Ash were starring in their own epic. The summer of 1995 offered a heady mix of tiny gigs in tiny places, followed by festivals in front of tens of thousands of people. From the Canterbury Penny Theatre to the Cork Feile, from T in the Park to the Liverpool Lomax, all roads led to the Reading Festival in August. Okay, so they were not on the main stage but in one of the tents, but this was where a rock band should be, the climax to the summer's gig-going. And Reading itself proved just how far Ash had come in such a short space of time.

Booked for the tent, by the time they came on, it was obvious they could have played second or third on the bill on the main stage. Certainly the tent could not accommodate all the rabid Ash fans who wanted a piece of the band. Never normally one to be worried by anything that was hardcore rock'n'roll, even Mark had his doubts about this show: 'We were playing in the *Melody Maker* tent and it was so packed there was just no movement in the front two-thirds of the crowd. You could see the pain on the people's faces as they were being crushed, but if we'd stopped playing, there'd probably have been a riot.'

Watching from a safe vantage point, the *NME*'s on the spot reporter said, 'The only other band capable of matching such scenes are the much touted bill-topping Foo

Fighters. [Ash provide] 150-second slices of angst drenched popcore in a vintage Buzzcocks style.' For the majority of those who attended Reading, it was painfully obvious that Ash were the hit of the weekend, that they were on the way out of the lower divisions of the pub and club circuit and off into the top flight, with Europe to come. Of course, not everyone was quite so ecstatic at the prospect, *Melody Maker* offering one of the most virulently anti-Ash reviews seen to date: 'The kids love Ash. Can't get enough of Ash. Kids, we need to talk. During Ash's set, a bespectacled twerp climbs the centre pole and dangles thereupon. As he revels in the greatest attention he will ever receive in his life, a clapping chant starts up directly beneath him. "Jump! Jump!" If he does jump, you idiots, he will land on you diving from a height of forty feet, driving you into the ground like an anvil hitting a tin-tack. This, kids, is Ash's audience. Think twice,' But even the *Maker*'s scribe was forced to admit, 'I know that the sworn enemies of cheery, grungy, punked over slurry rock will never stop Ash attaining the wild success that is surely theirs for the asking.'

Such an attitude was unusual but was becoming a little more prevalent in the media as people started to ask whether Ash – indeed any band – could be worthy of the riotous acclaim they were receiving. Their age became an increasing issue, much to Tim's utter frustration: 'I'd like people to be more interested in the music, though I admit that I'm only really starting to get the words together. Being young has worked both ways. Some people say, "They're teenagers? Brilliant!" But others say. "Teenagers? They must be shite!" And people can be very patronising. People keep saying, "God, you're really young to have had the success you have", but what they forget is that this line-up has been together for three years, far longer than Elastica. During that time, we've constantly had to fight to be taken seriously. If you're fifteen and tell a careers officer that you want to be a musician, the attitude is, "Oh, that's jolly nice but shouldn't you be thinking of something a little more practical?" No one believed, which actually worked in our favour because we were determined to prove them wrong.'

Those who were now criticising Ash for being too young had really missed the boat. They'd finished school. Rick was twenty, Tim and Mark eighteen-year-olds. If you are old enough to get married legally and get drunk, then you're certainly old enough to be in a successful rock'n'roll band. Just as important, that ignorant attitude was missing the seismic change that was taking place in Ash's songwriting. With 'Girl From Mars', Tim was emerging from his songwriting apprenticeship to the stage where he deserved to be taken seriously as an important talent. Ash as a whole deserved to have their reputation as a 'bouncy-castle Nirvana' reassessed, their specially produced Reading T-shirts, advertising 'Three Boy Hardcore Action' notwith-standing. Their song titles did them few favours, offering plenty of ammunition for those who wanted to trivialise them, but as Rick said, 'We're not trying to be daft. We just want to write really credible songs. We don't want to be tagged weird or anything like that.'

'Girl From Mars' was another stepping stone for the band, the most important to date. Look briefly at its achievements – number eleven in the charts, number eighteen in *NME*'s 'Singles of the Year' poll, *Select*'s number-ten single of the year. Yet these bare statistics tell little of the true story. 'Girl From Mars' represented a turning point in Tim's development as a songwriter, moving him away from the maudlin sense of loss felt in tracks like 'Uncle Pat' or 'Jack Names The Planets' to a more genuinely emotional, more personal, more honest articulation of that feeling. Where 'Jack Names The Planets' had been a successful songwriting exercise, this was a successful song-writing exorcism, Tim explaining, 'It's about summer and everything being caught up in the joy of youth. It makes me think about being on holiday, and being able to do what you want but knowing you'll be safe. Listening to it gives me a real feeling of confidence and self-assuredness and happiness. The idea's been knocking around for almost two years. I initially wrote the music, then came the verse and I finished the rest in the studio later. I actually wrote it after I split up with my first girlfriend. I went out with her for a year and it was such a perfect relationship at the time that I believed every relationship could be like that from then on. I guess I'm disillusioned now. I guess I was obsessed. But in the end, I just couldn't stand her indifference. It did my head in. I had such strong feelings for her but she always acted so coolly, so it was all a bit weird.'

If nothing else 'Girl From Mars' proved that Tim was a hopeless romantic and a kindred spirit of Robert Smith, both of which are really good signs for anyone embarking on a songwriting career. His evocation of the fleeting nature of life's best moments and the sense of desolation that can come in their wake was tender, touching and extremely impressive, the more so for its being set against the backing of a defiantly happy tune. Contrasts always work supremely well in pop music and that was something that Ash were quickly learning.

They were learning too the mechanics of the rock business just as quickly, ensuring that their material gained valuable exposure by appearing on film soundtracks, a lucrative business as well as a commercially sound one. In August, Tim told the press that 'we're on the soundtrack of a movie called *Angus*. ["Jack Names The Planet" and "Kung Fu" were included in the Kathy Bates film.] The best thing about it is the soundtrack is almost bound to sell a million because it is got some Green Day exclusives on it. And all those Green Day fans are bound to like Ash.' Keep those cash registers whirring . . .

The touring never stopped however and with the Reading triumph in the bag, it was back to more prosaic venues such as Manchester University, where Mark Beaumont of the *NME* caught their show and was quick to notice the difference between the old and the new material: '"Jack Names The Planets" and "Sneakers" race in fresh from a Mega City Four bland rock masterclass. The nerve tingling power is there all right, but where are the tunes? [But] there is a rattling, glorious desperation in tunes like the awesome "Kung Fu" which goes further in exorcising the frustrations of Teenage than just keeping your teeth nice and clean.'

Going out on the road might seem exciting, but a lot of the time, a band has to make its own entertainment. Mark was especially good at that. 'I got a real bollocking in the middle of the tour for going for it every night. After ten days, I was wrecked. I couldn't even walk. So I got a right slapping,' Mark's fun generally came out of a bottle, for as he noted, following his illness, 'I don't do drugs any more. What drugs that do go on are very tame. I don't get along with them. But I'm not missing the party. I drink myself unconscious almost every day. I think that because for a while I did sink so low, I've probably got a better chance now of keeping it together.' Among Mark's more glorious escapades came when he walked into a hotel kitchen freezer, so drunk that he did not know where he was. One blast of cold air and the inevitable happened: 'I ended up pissing on the frozen turkeys.' An interesting method of thawing them out, but not one to be recommended next Christmas.

So confident were Ash by this stage that they were ready and willing to release another new single in October, supporting it with the most cursory of UK tours which ended at the Astoria, where the *NME* accurately remarked, 'Ash are already frighteningly close to a "Greatest Hits" set.' With six singles behind them, four of which had charted, that was a perceptive comment which boded well for the future. The only downside to Ash's irresistible rise to the top came off stage. Rick had been set upon in a Belfast pub for committing the heinous crime of wearing eye-liner, though this gave the rest of the Ash entourage the chance to mint a new Rick story, the tale of how he became 'rock'n'roll', as told to, and by, *Vox*'s Steven Wells: 'Rick is the least rock'n'roll person in rock'n'roll, the sombre, serious, straight As student cursed with a physique closer to John Major [remember him? He used to be Prime Minister] than Johnny Rotten. He has retaliated by reinventing himself as a cross between Andy Warhol and Oliver Reed. The best version [of how Rick got cool] is he walked into a pub in drag and got battered by a moron who broke his totally punk rock milk bottle bottom geekspex and the rest of the band made him go and get cool new ones.' This was the latest in the line of humiliations bestowed on Rick. Tim recalled, 'We dressed him up in a fairy suit one Christmas. That was good . . . Ru-Paul is a role model for Rick,' while later Rick had to shave all his hair after Mark had cut it; 'I had bald patches and step marks all over my head.' Nor did Rick have the greatest success with band followers. Tim recounted, 'One time, this girl asked Rick outside. He thought he was well in, but then this other girl turned up and she started snogging her instead,' Understandably perhaps, Rick was not enamoured by the groupie phenomenon: 'Actually, being told "I want it now big boy" by a total stranger can be very intimidating. Worse still is when they turn round afterwards and say "You're not as good as that bloke from Northern Uproar".'

If Rick had a pretty mixed time of it, Mark's fall from

grace was even more dramatic. Hanging from a balcony in Nottingham's Rock City, he managed to fall and shatter his ankle. This of course gave him the perfect excuse to drink more in order to numb the pain. The drinking never stopped, nor did the touring. There is a limit to how long you can safely maintain that lethal combination, and the limit was fast approaching.

7.

KILLER BANANAS

Just as the release of 'Girl From Mars' had upped the stakes, so too did the unveiling of their 'Angel Interceptor' single, the title taken from the *Captain Scarlet* TV show. It was a further example of Tim's changing lyrical focus for he said that this time the song was about missing someone sexually. 'We're not just being frivolous and fun, our lyrics are about missing people which is the kind of thing I can be attracted to, that feeling of melancholy,' said Tim. The vast, lush romanticism of the opening backing vocals – a little let down by a pretty ordinary vocal performance from Tim – showed the ever increasing scope of their ambition. In this one single they invoked the spirit of those great harmonies trademarked by The Beach Boys in the 1960s, the sense of wonder of R.E.M.'s 'Star Me Kitten' from *Automatic For The People* was captured in those lovely backing vocals while the overall sense of attack and the final spiralling guitar riff was right out of the Queen catalogue. And yet the whole thing was still unmistakably Ash – maybe it was the off-beat nature of title and lyrics, maybe it was the exuberance with which they played the song. Whatever it was, Ash had established their own sound, and all in a matter of eighteen months, a remarkable achievement. They were a hit on their own terms. Influenced yes, but not slavish copyists.

'Angel Interceptor' charted at number fourteen, further proof that Ash were here to stay. It picked up the now obligatory 'Single of the Week' honours in *NME*, and an appropriate review: 'This record reminds me of everything. Belting along in fine style with too many guitars on it, clever fiddly riffs here and there and at last the singer's frankly appalling voice is growing into the band's frankly bizarre melodies. When they are grown to full manhood, they will surely be huge stars. Excellent.' Even *The Times* got in on the act, with David Sinclair having this to say: 'Recalls the punky overdrive of The Pixies. Using images of space travel as a metaphor for romantic travel is not an entirely original concept but the simply stated theme at the heart of the song combines with the emotional uplift of the chorus to sweep all before it.' All was not sweetness and light however, for *Vox* felt that 'whoever signed this band should have their ears removed'.

The release of 'Angel Interceptor' also featured one of those bizarre accidents that seem destined to dog the band forever. According to Rick, 'Our manager's assistant sent some copies of the CD off to us – one each – and mine didn't turn up. I was going to phone up to tell her it had got lost in the post. Then my brother came to my room while I was in bed and said, "The police are here. They want to speak to you. They have got a CD".' The parcel had been addressed wrongly and had ended up at the home of a security officer who had previously been threatened by the paramilitaries. The package, simply addressed to 'Rick' had had the postcode scored through and looked suspicious, the more so since the officer in question did not have a CD player. By the time the CD finally got to Rick, it had been X-rayed and been given the once-over by the bomb squad.

Such problems merely reminded people that Ash were a band from Northern Ireland, with all the implications that that carries. Where some felt that using titles like 'Girl From Mars' or 'Angel Interceptor' was needlessly foolish, there was also a suspicion that they were ducking the issues of Northern Irish politics, deliberately avoiding confronting the realities that surrounded them. In one sense that was true, for as Tim argued, 'I don't think I'll ever write about the troubles. It's very hard to write about without adopting a high moral attitude. It sounds bad, but it doesn't really affect us much and no one really understands it any more. It is just me being totally apathetic. I was born in 1977 so I grew up with the troubles, but I've no interest whatsoever in politics or religion. There have been a couple of times where my ignorance has nearly got me into trouble though. I was driving round Belfast one day and got lost in Sandy Row where there are all these famous Loyalist murals. It looked like a perfectly normal estate to me but if I'd asked for directions, I'd probably have been shot. Then, we were playing the Penny Farthing in Belfast and a bloke came in and told us to turn it down. We asked him why and he just pulled a load of bullets out of his pocket.'

Tim's antipathy towards the sectarian nature of Ulster's politics is understandable. After all, if you are a native of Northern Ireland and have grown up with the troubles pretty much on your doorstep, you have to evolve a way of living with it, of dealing with it on a day-to-day basis. If you make it the sole focus of your life, you either go mad or join one of the terrorist groups. In some respects, the majority of the ordinary people of Northern Ireland probably take less notice of events there than the people on the mainland do, unless it directly involves them. For an English visitor to Belfast, it is a real shock to see soldiers walking the streets. For a local, it is everyday life.

One good reason for not writing about the troubles is the difficulty of summing up hundreds of years of conflict in two and a half minutes. Perhaps Tim was being modest when he said 'lots of people have already written about it a lot better than I ever could', but he would be right in thinking he could not do the subject justice, for who could? Equally, any such song could only be seen as exploiting the pain of the people who suffer year in, year out. There have been enough crass attempts to do that in the past – remember those urban guerrillas The Clash mounting the barricades for a photo opportunity before flying straight back to London? As a politics student, you would be forgiven for expecting Rick to have the most to say on the subject, but he was wise enough to keep his own counsel, pointing out the stupidity of trying to resolve conflict in song by referring to 'Zombie', one of the more famous songs about the troubles in recent years: 'I think Downpatrick's share of the guns and bombs and tanks are in Limerick. They must be because The Cranberries are singing about 'em.' Rick's attitude, not to trivialise what is, after all, a civil war, can be the only sensible line to take.

Of course, no one from Northern Ireland can avoid the realities in a country where simply drawing breath is a political act. Every time Ash attracted any bad publicity, they 'got a lot of shit from Unionists saying we are disgraceful' according to Mark. Their attitude is a particularly personal one, strongly anti-violence, setting an example, however inadvertently, that others could follow. Tim proudly points to, 'Shows we've done in Belfast, kids of both religions and sides just enjoying themselves together. That is more than a lot of politicians have done. At least we're bringing people together. And look at the road crew. We're a Proddy band and all of our crew are Fenians! So I reckon we do enough without writing a song about the whole thing. We've seen some really scummy places while we've been on tour that just make you realise how much Northern Ireland has got going for it. It just needs people to wise up.'

There was plenty of opportunity to see the rest of the world for the band toured incessantly right up to Christmas and beyond, ending a triumphant year on Prince's Street in Edinburgh, playing the Hogmanay Party. First real visits to America and the Far East were included, giving them time to run up a bill of almost £8,000 for smashing up a

Japanese hotel room. As Mark ruefully recounted later, 'It costs too much to smash things up. I don't do it to let off steam, I do it because it's fun. Letting fire extinguishers off is a fetish but it's an expensive wee thing even if it does give you a rush. I've still got an outstanding bill of about three grand to pay back to the tour account from previous escapades.'

With the onset of 1996 came the chance to get down to work on the vital début album, breaking only to play the Brat Awards in January, *Melody Maker*'s Everett True reporting that 'Ash are too damn happy for my liking; what do they have to be twisted and angry and fucked up about?' With a clutch of glittering singles behind them, they knew full well that it would be the album that would make it clear if they could make the grade here and abroad.

With Owen Morris on board, they retained the same team that had made three great singles in a row and so the scene was set for further successes. The first fruits of these new labours came with the release of 'Goldfinger' in April 1996. Straight in at number five, many saw this as some kind of bolt from the blue, but clearly they had not been paying close enough attention to the way Ash had been evolving in recent months, a fact recognised when they won the *Hot Press* award for Best Irish Band in March. In *NME* 'Goldfinger' was credited as the sign which 'reveals the Irish threesome to be in possession of hitherto concealed smoochy, sophisticated instincts', while *Melody Maker*'s Daniel Booth felt that it 'makes it obvious that Ash are the missing link between The Buzzcocks and Nirvana'. But that much had been obvious for months. For Tim, it was a big turning point: 'We proved we could do proper music as well as throwaway adrenalin pop. I think it is the best thing we've done.' The crunching guitar intro was clearly influenced by Nirvana but the sense of aching melancholia at the very heart of the song was all Tim's own work, a further refinement of his lyrical obsession.

With 'Goldfinger' came a host of problems. In the round of press interviews that accompanied its release, we were treated to the details of Mark's previous love affair with drugs, the details of his illness and, in a throwaway comment, his one-off use of heroin. As Tim put it, 'Mark admitted to taking heroin and hating it and the next thing you know half the country's reading about the "Heroin Hell Of Teen Ash Rocker: My Drugs Shame".' Besieged by the local press, even Tim's mother Rosalind had to issue a statement on behalf of the band: 'We know the boys are pretty sound, we know what they are really like. They're much more sensible than they are portrayed in the music press. You cannot go off the rails and be successful in any business,' a pretty reasonable comment. Amid all the media generated hysteria, one comment from Mark was scarcely picked up on. It was about his state of health, and bear in mind this was more than twelve months after he had been hospitalised, 'It's been a very slow recovery. I'm still on tablets. Valium and Novrac, which is a bit like Prozac. I still get headaches all the time but the tablets are sorting me out.' So far so good, but Mark's health was still fragile. In addition, he and the others had been under the severe strain of piecing together their make or break album for three months and so were understandably exhausted. Why then was this their forthcoming schedule?:

7th May – 8th July. Thirty-five shows in eleven countries all over Europe in sixty-three days.

14th July – 16th August. Twenty-seven shows in America in thirty-four days.

22nd – 25th August. Three festivals in four days – Oslo, Dronton, Reading.

26th August – 20th September. Time off!

21st September – 22nd December. Sixty-six shows in ninety-three days in Thailand, Japan, Australia, New Zealand, America and Canada.

Taking away the three weeks off in September, that was 131 shows in 194 days, where most of the days off would involve travelling of some kind. If you were in the best health of your life, that would look daunting. If, on the other hand, you were a rock'n'roll band fresh out of the studio, exhausted and looking to live up to your hell-raising reputation, it was almost suicidal. Trying to be phlegmatic about it all, Tim merely noted that, 'We volunteered for it. We're just the band who can't say no.' It might have served them better if they had.

The 'Goldfinger' press might have centred on Mark's lifestyle, but other issues cropped up too. Suddenly, Ash were 'Britpop', saddled with another movement. Tim was having none of that though: 'It's just a label. I guess technically we are Britpop 'cos we're from Northern Ireland but I don't want to be part of it. I carry about 120 CDs around with me and Oasis are the only Britpop band I'm into. I wouldn't ever listen to Blur.' While trying to push Ash into the Britpop corner on one hand, others were criticising them for not being an authentically Irish band. Rick was amazed by the assertion: 'We've been accused of denying our Irishness which is fucking ludicrous. What do they want me to do? Buy a bodhrán and start going to sessions? I don't care about fiddle players and uilleann pipers. Our Irish influences are Therapy? and The Undertones, not big beardy blokes singing about maidens fair and true.' His annoyance was understandable for an English band would not suffer the same treatment; Liam Gallagher is rarely quizzed over his apparent lack of enthusiasm for morris dancing, for instance.

Once the album came out, most of those critics were silenced. *1977* was a stunning triumph. Not every song was a clear winner, but as a debut record with all the inconsistencies that inevitably implies, it was remarkable. One commentator, Ed Ward, wrote, 'Ash never forget the primary purpose of making this music is to entertain. [Their] romanticism makes me think of The Beach Boys, that sort of doomed sentimentalism that strikes such a chord,' Rick was thrilled by the review handed out by *CMJ* magazine in America: 'It said I was Ash's secret weapon which I find quite amusing. Half the review said the songs were good and the rest just talked about how great the drums were.' Yet some reviews were less than kind. In

Melody Maker, Victoria Segal wrote a stringent attack on the band and what she perceived to be the anodyne nature of the material: 'You can rub up against their buzzy songs for the odd pleasure fix without any danger they'll twine their way round your heart. Or mind . . . shut someone in a room for a week with nothing but a copy of *1977* and chances are they'll emerge with a huge grin and absolutely no conversation . . . Ash are disingenuous lads. Don't believe for a minute they're three nice guileless boys, all wide-eyed wonder and tunes as bright and sugary as penny sweets.' Commenting on the perfect timing for such a release, she went on, 'Summer likes songs that fade out in woozy euphoria and bring to mind Danny and Sandy soaring away in the car at the end of *Grease* . . . never aspires to be anything beyond 'My Guy' indie, boys next door making music for girls next door. It is as exciting as school discos promised to be but ultimately as fulfilling. You could call it harmless if that didn't sound so damn pernicious.' But these sentiments were unnecessarily harsh. Ash songs rarely have the happy endings she implied, for example, and were considerably more barbed. Falling into the trap of looking at the fresh-faced youths who made the music rather than the music they made, Segal and others missed the increasingly gritty songs the band were producing.

Tim had pointed out the coming changes going into the recording, 'So far the songs have been all about innocence and belief. You feel secure when you're at home. You don't have to worry about anything and you're completely free. Someone will always be there to look after you. So even though you may feel lonely, you're not alone. That feeling of wonder was one of the things that caused me to write. I don't feel a lot of that any more. All those songs that came up before, they weren't premeditated, it was all very natural. It is tough trying to think where I'm going now. There'll probably be a lot more sex and stuff, not so sweet.'

That was clearly the case on a song like 'Oh Yeah', a sumptuous song of summer, of the last day of school and the bittersweet mix of anticipation and trepidation. Romantic, it was sultry and sexy too, that Beatlesque string section complementing the song perfectly, Tim's Cure-like scatting in the background a new feature in the mix. If you sought any one example of their new maturity, 'Oh Yeah' provided it. When it came out as a single in September, *NME* made it Single of the Week and went on: 'The monster munching tune which marches through the melodic wastelands stabbing at the Ballad Dragon with a sharp stick until the Ballad Dragon cracks open and spews forth a Jazz Orange-tinted gooey fluid approximating pop genius. Impeccable.'

Inevitably, the singles made up much of the best material, but the record was studded with other highlights. 'I'd Give you Anything' and 'Let It Flow' might have been uninspired grunge workouts that suggested they were merely filler material, the closing 'Darkside Lightside' suggested a flirtation with the classic rock genre hinted at earlier on 'Lose Control', itself, 'Not a true story,' according to Tim, 'but it's about sleeping with someone else's girlfriend.' 'Darkside Lightside' opened in manic fashion with Iron Maiden guitars blazing, but was transformed into a triumphal procession by its close with the return of those romantic backing vocals for one last blast, with the closing guitar figure reminiscent of Pink Floyd of all people. When Ash play the arenas, this will be the one that gets the cigarette lighters held aloft.

Other influences were apparent too, some unlikely. The melody of the old classic 'Strangers In The Night' was lifted for 'Lost In You', which *Melody Maker*'s Ian Watson termed 'an emotional coming of age, real life magnified tenfold'. U2 circa *Achtung Baby* were in vogue for 'Innocent Smile' and 'Gone The Dream' crammed in The Beatles as band and as solo artists too, from 'Dear Prudence' through to Wings via 'My Sweet Lord'. But this list of influences is just a part of the tale. Ash were recognisably themselves, though their devotion to Nirvana bordered on the slavish at times. For much of the record's duration however, the songs crackled with excitement and a healthy degree of innovation. Most important, they seemed to have an intuitive grasp of the difference between playing a song live and playing it in the studio. Live, they could rock out, playing everything at breakneck speed. On the album, they gave themselves room to breathe, stretching the songs, pacing the record, attacking when necessary, relaxing where the songs required. To pick a fault would be invidious, but it has to be pointed out that Ash were at their best when they let a glorious chorus do the talking rather than trying to bludgeon the audience into submission with lo-fi noise.

Tim felt sure the record would be a hit: 'We were dead confident at the time. We knew it was really good and it'd do well because "Angel Interceptor" and "Girl From Mars" sold 80,000 copies each.' But even he must have been amazed by pre-sales of 122,000 and a chart entry at number one. It started a rush of motormouth quips that turned Tim into one of the best interviewees around. For example, when John Lydon claimed *1977* as a tribute to The Sex Pistols, Tim's response was curt, 'The Pistols mean fuck all to anyone under thirty. The reason we called our album *1977* is because that is the year two of us were born. If John Lydon reckons we are paying him some sort of tribute, then he's more senile than I thought.'

As the record hit the racks, confidence went sky high. No longer one to undersell himself, Tim claimed, 'I can write the songs. I've proved it. Halfway through recording the album, we scrapped a load of stuff because we were writing better material. I'm not worried about anything. You know what I'm gonna do with my gold disc? I'm gonna have sex on it.' In spite of looking forward to a summer of picking shards of glass out of his backside, things quickly turned sour on planet Ash.

Internal difficulties had surfaced during recording, understandably enough. The pressure was on and they had to deliver. Tim recalled, 'It was a completely insane three months. We were only fucked up a couple of nights. The rest of the time we were working. We weren't gonna let it go until we were completely happy.' According to Mark, 'About two months in, we started hiding away from the rest of the world, getting a bit crazy, doing nothing but recording and writing and drinking, just the six of us there for three months. "Sick Party" came out of that. One night they were all on acid and I wasn't feeling well, so we thought that I could be sick, we'd get a microphone to it and we could put it in the background, just to add to the record.' These sessions resemble those The Cure held for *Pornography* at the point they were debilitatingly paranoid and really going off the rails, holing up in their management's office, living in tents and constructing mountains out of used beer cans, with no sense of perspective. They then went off on tour and went slowly mad, taking their frustration out on one another with acts of violence, though no one ever picked on Robert Smith, the band leader. The instinctive drive for perfection can create great music but it can also be extremely self-destructive.

Tim now admits that during the recording, 'I was exhausted and we were pretty depressed, pretty burned out. It was a psychotic schedule and it just got too much.' Mark realised that things were not well with his colleague, commenting three months after its release, 'He put his whole soul into that record. But I've known him for years. He's recovering now and I know he'll be fine. People weren't born to deal with this whole fame thing when it gets so mad. One girl threatened to jump off a building if he didn't talk to her.' For Mark and Rick, recording was less intense but as the focal point of the group, the buck always stops with Tim. In addition, Rick and Mark had other things to do in order to lighten the tension. Mark had helped set up X-Wing Records in Belfast and in the spring of 1996, they released their first record, a sampler entitled 'Laugh Hard At The Absurdly Evil'. One band, Sneaker, featured Rick on guitar, Mark on bass, along with Barry Peak of Backwater as vocalist and Shaun Robinson on drums. Their contribution, 'Easter Island', was actually Ash's song 'Sneaker' but with new lyrics. Such extra-curricular activities gave fresh enthusiasm for their work with Ash and helped diffuse the tension they were feeling.

Nevertheless, around this time, the first rumours of a split in the band began to surface. Tim made the necessary diplomatic denials, saying they were 'the product of someone's really over-active imagination', a line he sticks with to this day. Mark however was not so sanguine, 'It really got so bad that we did nearly split.' The pressures that had been mounting for month upon month were finally starting to get to the band. Tim in particular found dealing with his position especially hard: 'Everything had got like a crazed endurance test or something. I got so paranoid and depressed about how little control I had over my life that I thought about giving it all up. It was mainly trying to come to terms with being a pop star. I wondered if it was good for me or if it'd just mess me up. I think in my head, I thought the album was a really big deal and once I'd done it, I'd be really happy and sorted and everything would be great. But I found out it didn't really mean anything.'

Having put so much into something that suddenly seemed futile, it is not surprising that the world fell in around Tim. Had there been a chance to stop and reflect properly on all the band's achievements to date, perspective would have been regained. As it was, it seemed like Ash were on military service, packed up and shipped out to wave the flag in foreign climes. Tim admitted that he lost confidence in himself and what he was doing, a point poignantly made by the loneliness expressed in the song 'Lost In You' on *1977*: 'After the album came out and we started touring, I just couldn't sleep. I was having really bad dreams, freaking out and just lying in bed crying. I think it was because of everyone telling me how great the album was and I thought it was shit . . . we formed this band to get away from conventional lifestyles but so much shit goes on you lose sight of it. Right now, I'd love to sleep in my own bed and get fed by my mum. You can waste your youth doing this. We're under a lot of pressure for nineteen-year-olds, and I miss not giving a fuck. We're on a full-on schedule and things can get very hardcore . . . we're not self-destructive no matter what the tabloids say. We just live an exhausting lifestyle . . . I do sometimes wonder if we should call it quits before someone gets really fucked up.'

Having a number one is not necessarily the answer to all your prayers then – as the old saying goes, beware of what you wish for in case you get it. While the band were going through this inner turmoil, they were, somewhat inevitably, taking their frustrations out on the music and on themselves, drinking at a rate that even they had not managed before. Some hotels took precautions when visited by the rampaging Downpatrick hoards, Tim being dumbstruck when 'We checked into a hotel room in Norway and we found out that our three rooms had had the televisions taken out of them. How can we be expected to be rock'n'roll when people take precautions like that?'

Even so, they were still pretty rock'n'roll. The music took a pounding, with live shows getting louder and louder, faster and faster. The contrast was illustrated by two starkly different reviews. The first comes from Daniel Booth of *Melody Maker*, reflecting on the London Forum show of 24 May: 'The sound of drunken teenage parties, a world populated by fun seeking sixth formers where happy boyfriends go out with their happy girlfriends. It is a soap opera with a cast of thou . . . millions. At least. Flirting with both the energy of punk and the ferocity of grunge, they are "proper" teenagers playing shagging music.' All at this stage was comparatively normal. Six weeks later on 1 July, they played the SFX in Dublin. Presented with a platinum disc for sales of *1977* in Ireland, Tim promptly hurled the award into the crowd. Afterwards, Ian Watson filed this very different critique for *NME*: 'A raging rock beast high on ear-piercing screams and determined to show they've made the leap from geeks to Gods. Tim, in particular, comes across as a surly axe-hero, a battle-scarred rogue with his adult status now embodied in an invulnerable Jimmy Page stance. Mark, meanwhile, stands right at the edge of the stage, psyching out the crowd, a threat rather than a kindred spirit. The impetuous pop buzz of the Ash legend is being given a nasty new dimension. Ash's latest phase is not a natural progression but an inspired and unique leap into an unexpected future.'

This personality change bordered on the schizophrenic, for Ash were no longer the purveyors of perfect pop but were instead a snapping, vicious hard rock band. It reflected the tensions that they were working through, each teetering on the edge, brought there by a mix of over indulgence and over work. For both Tim and Rick, the crunch seemed to come in mid-June when the hectic schedule went completely haywire. Tim recalls, 'We played a gig in Austria, flew to a video shoot in Great Yarmouth and then played *Later* with Jools Holland for the BBC. I was at serious breaking point.' For Rick, it was potentially even more serious. 'I almost had a nervous breakdown at *Later*. We'd done some speed the night before to stay up and as we were playing the songs my heart was beating way too fast. I finished the song and I was just sitting there with my head in my hands, hyperventilating with heart palpitations and everything.'

In spite of these warning signs, Ash carried on pretty much as before, living life to the absolute maximum and well beyond. Pausing only to turn down the offer of an Oasis support slot, they descended upon Leipzig, playing a festival headlined by David Bowie. Mark was distinctly unimpressed: 'I drank two bottles of gin, pushed over the security and tried to get into the tower to do David Bowie's lights. I was just trying to liven things up because he was shite.' Not content with that, Mark's next good idea was to try and get on stage in an attempt to wake up the thin white dork but got rugby tackled by a slightly more sober Tim who thought this might not be such a good career move.

For his pains, Tim was set upon by security who thought he was a fan attacking Mark.

Tim and Rick had reined things in little after the scares of the *Later* show, but Mark was still in his element. The aggression they channelled into their stage show also won new converts in the States – indeed, their coruscating displays were the ideal way of capturing the attention of audiences unfamiliar with their music. They certainly impressed *Addicted To Noise*'s Claire Kleinedler who wrote that Ash were 'a live act that made me want to jump up and down and just break into fits of reckless abandon ... Hamilton is so in touch with his instrument that he can swoop all over the stage as if in a drunken haze [what do you mean, "as if"?], nearly head-butt his bandmates and still crank it out with skilled precision ... spell-binding, sweat-inducing, heart-pumping.'

Of course, all good things must come to an end. Sadly in the rock business, they often come to an end only when a performer has drunk him or herself into an early grave. Mark was clearly threatening to go the same way, Tim noting, 'It was totally out of control at one point. Mark was putting away a bottle of gin a night. That was pretty gruesome.' Rick also recounted stories of Mark's excess, though they may have been a little exaggerated in the telling: 'We were playing in St Louis and Mark had drunk about a litre of gin beforehand. Suddenly his amp breaks down and he takes the hump, so he kicks the tour manager, shouts at the guitar tech, "I'm going to punch you tomorrow", drinks about three bottles of gin and doesn't make it off stage at the end of the show. He was lying flat on his arm unconscious while everyone was taking the gear off.' This particular outburst left him with a dead arm, but that was a nothing compared with the final straw which came in Los Angeles.

Following another strenuous gig, according to Tim, Mark was attacked by a banana. 'He was holding it in a phallic position and pretending to chop it up with a knife and, being a complete dickhead, he sliced his finger open. He had to go to hospital and get twelve stitches. It was after the show, about midnight. It is his way of relaxing.' In the cold light of the following day, everyone realised that rather than having a jagged wound on his hand, the bass player might now be minus a finger or two, which would certainly cramp his style. It was time for the partying to come to a halt. What had been endearing two years earlier was now plain stupid, and it was even starting to weaken their popularity. When 'Oh Yeah' came out a single in September, it was greeted with this *Melody Maker* review: 'Charmlessly amateurish and the singing's excruciating. I mean, what's so bloody vital or even youthful about getting drunk and setting off a couple of fire extinguishers? My uncle does that everyday and the kids in his street just think he's sad.'

Thankfully, Mark's injury was repairable, but it was the final warning for the band. They could be forgiven for their life of stupidity given the burdens placed upon them, but that would have been no consolation had Mark lost his career or even worse. The aftermath was a combined decision to calm things down. As Tim put it, 'We have moments of madness now instead of moments of seriousness. We had a meeting and we sorted it out. We basically hadn't stopped from touring to doing the album and back to touring again. The schedule was mental and we just cracked up. In the end, touring America helped us put everything into perspective, because we're virtually unknown there. Before, we went at things with all guns blazing, not really sure of where we were at, but I think we've changed. Basically, I think we're a lot more grown up and a lot more confident but you have to be careful when you're on the road. You sort of lose touch with who you really are, all your roots are gone, you're in the middle of nowhere. Everything changes every day.'

With a semblance of normality restored, the remainder of 1996 passed off in comparatively sedate fashion, the band trekking around America in support of Stabbing Westward and then Weezer, triumphantly finishing the year with a huge headline gig at The Point in Dublin. Most importantly of all, they were able to turn down support slots in the States with U2 and Bush, having already ignored the advances of The Sex Pistols, Metallica, Bon Jovi and Def Leppard. As Tim noted, 'It's so easy. Thirty minutes a night is simple. But if we'd done that, we'd never get a new album made and new music's much more important.' With priorities intact, Ash could look to the future with confidence once again.

8.

BETTER AND BETTER

Waking up in January 1997 must have been pretty good if you were a member of Ash. You had survived everything that 1996 had had to throw at you and come out stronger for it. Sales of tickets for your gigs at London's Astoria in February were going through the roof, such that the 'Ashtoria' residency stretched to five sold-out shows – 'we could have done Wembley Arena,' admitted Tim, 'but that would have been naff.' Better yet, here was a whole month without gigs, giving you the chance to unwind, write a little and enjoy yourself a lot. With only February's European shows ahead of you, the year looked like a good one. So it has proved thus far. Tim started to fill his new London flat, the band were asked to write a song for Ewan McGregor's new movie, they picked up the *Hot Press* award for Best Irish Band and Best Irish Single with 'Oh Yeah' and performed live with Neil Hannon of The Divine Comedy. Everything was back on an even keel and the future could be faced with confidence.

The February gigs were blistering affairs, all the good humour and verve back in situ after the troubles of the previous summer. So content were they, they even agreed to play a support slot, though one with a difference, and for one night only at the Astoria Gay club. As Tim explained, 'We've been offered support slots by U2, Oasis, Blur, Pearl Jam, Radiohead and we said no to them all. But we said yes to Michelle Gayle. That officially makes us the coolest band on the planet!' Introducing themselves with the words 'so many men and just us three boys', they romped through Abba's 'Does Your Mother Know?', Smokey Robinson's 'Get Ready' and Dusty Springfield's 'I Only Want To Be With You'.

Impressive though the Astoria gigs were, the focus for February was on the release on a new Ash album, *Live At The Wireless*. The official line was that this was a bootleg album but one with which they were so happy, that they would help to promote it. That was a wise decision, indicative of their more relaxed state of mind. No longer so precious, Ash were willing to let things go, to concentrate on what they wanted to do and ignore the trappings of rock stardom. *Live At The Wireless*, was recorded at Triple J studios in Sydney in October 1996, and it proved that by then things had started to get back to normal. The good tempered run through of classics and covers was Ash at their best, up on stage and loving every minute of it; Tim's introduction before 'Petrol' was just like a kid in his bedroom, playing his tennis racquet in front of the mirror – that was either an example of him laughing at himself piss-take or a genuine example of their excitable naiveté, either of which were perfectly fine.

As the title suggested, the album was recorded in a radio studio without an audience and as such there was a strange mixture of atmosphere, raw power and intimacy, as though they were back in the clubs again where you could see the whites of their eyes. Fast, punky, a po-goers delight, this was a back to basics album, one which highlighted all that was good about them – melody, aggression, angst, tunes, power, sense of humour. That humour was shown in the sleevenotes which were not the contents of an Ash flight-case but lifted from Hunter S. Thompson's *Fear And Loathing In Las Vegas*. It also came in the final track, 'A Clear Invitation To The Dance', featuring roadie Leif. Just as *1977* featured a long silence before 'Sick Party', there was five minutes of nothing before the track was repeated in a different version. Having sucked you in, made you expect another 'Sick Party', this was a much wittier outcome.

Ian Watson was typically enthusiastic in the course of his *Melody Maker* review, pointing out, 'As a behind the scenes glimpse into the whole process, this is invaluable. You can almost picture the broad grin on Tim Wheeler's face as he forgets this is just a job and lets the heat-seeking vitality of "Kung Fu" sweep him off his feet.' In the *NME*, Mark Beaumont was a little less taken, but still enjoyed the record as warts and all Ash rather than embellished Ash: 'At last, they are demanding their innocence back. To the purist, this is the closest we'll come to seeing their bare bones and raw flesh, unglossed by studio polish for some time. The glaring mistakes and the studio tomfoolery remind us why we found these vivacious young tykes so charming in the first place.'

By the first week in March, all the hype was out of the way and Ash were faced with filling a blank slab of vinyl with their new songs. The prospects look much brighter than they did in July 1996, for the band have now come to terms with their celebrity and are now focusing once more on the music. What can we expect? Even Rick is not certain: 'The first album sounds pretty punky but we're changing, listening to lots of rock and stuff, the Stooges, Bowie, The Rolling Stones, quite a lot of old music. There'll probably still be a punky edge but I don't think we fit into the traditional sort of punk thing, there is more going on. A lot of melody.'

This album will tell us all a lot more about Ash, as Tim accepts, 'If I'm a really good songwriter which I think I might be, we'll find out on this next record. I don't really wanna rush it because it's really important. We'll just take it easy and wait 'til we've had some time off before we start getting into it. It'll be better, stronger, more dark and mysterious, not so poppy but still very melodic. I look back on some of the lyrics from 1977 and they now seem a little too sickly sweet for me. I won't do them like that again. My understanding of music has increased.'

Certainly, they have had a wealth of experience since finishing the last album and it will be interesting to see if and how that filters through into the recording process. The raw material is clearly there if they wish to tap into it.

Once the record does come out, we in the UK will see a lot less of Ash than we have been used to. The second album will see a real onslaught on the American market. Tim is realistic about the possibilities: 'The only way to break there is to go across, be unassuming and work your bollocks off. Being on the front page of a British music magazine means fuck all on the other side of the Atlantic. We spent half of 1996 in the US and it was important for us to do that. We wanted to start making an impact over there and that takes time. We're starting to build up a fan base, but I think it's going to take until our next record.'

If Ash are going to become an important band, one to rank with U2, The Smiths, The Beatles or bands of that ilk, they really have only just begun. If that is their goal, then in 2005, as Rick celebrates his thirtieth birthday, we will all be looking back at *1977* as a quaint, if promising start, a bit funny, embarrassing in parts, brilliant in others. Six or seven albums into their career, people may well wonder how it was they made a record as patchy as *1977*. That is the challenge that awaits Ash – to make their first album look average.

It does not daunt Tim: 'I think we'll be doing this for quite some time yet. We've a long way to go to reach our peak because we're still developing all the time. We're getting better and better. That's one of the good things about the fact that we started so young. We've a lot of time left.'

UK DISCOGRAPHY

SINGLES

JACK NAMES THE PLANETS
Jack Names The Planets / Don't Know.
La La Land Records.
February 1994.

PETROL
Petrol / The Little Pond / A Message From Oscar Wilde And
Patrick The Brewer / Things.
Infectious Records.
August 1994.

UNCLE PAT
Uncle Pat / Different Today / Hulk Hogan Bubble Bath.
Infectious Records.
October 1984.
Chart: 38.

KUNG FU
Kung Fu / Day Of The Triffids / Luther Ingo's Star Cruiser.
Infectious Records.
March 1995.
Chart: 57.

GIRL FROM MARS
Girl From Mars / Astral Conversations With Toulouse-Lautrec / Cantina Band.
Infectious Records.
July 1995.
Chart: 11.

ANGEL INTERCEPTOR
Angel Interceptor / 5 a.m. Eternal / Give Me Some Truth.
Infectious Records.
October 1995.
Chart: 14.

GET READY
Get Ready / Zero Zero.
Fantastic Plastic Records.
December 1995.
(Limited edition seven-inch single).

GOLDFINGER
Goldfinger / I Need Somebody / Sneaker / Get Ready.
Infectious Records.

April 1996.
Chart: 5.

OH YEAH
Oh Yeah / T Rex / Everywhere Is All Around / Does Your Mother Know?
Infectious Records.
June 1996.
Chart: 6.

BARBIE 7"
I Only Want To Be With You / Devil's Haircut / Kung Fu.
Barbie Records.
February 1997.
(Limited edition seven-inch for fan club members, issued through the mail and at Ashtoria shows).

ALBUMS

TRAILER
Season / Message From Oscar Wilde And Patrick The Brewer / Jack Names The Planets / Intense Thing / Uncle Pat / Message From Mr.Waterman / Get out / Petrol / Obscure Thing.
Infectious Records.
Produced by Mark Waterman & Tim Russell.
October 1994.

1977

Lose Control / Goldfinger / Girl From Mars / I'd Give You Anything / Gone The Dream / Kung Fu / Oh Yeah / Let it Flow / Angel Interceptor / Lost In you / Darkside Lightside / Sick Party.

Infectious Records.

Produced by Owen Morris & Ash.

May 1996.

Chart: 1.

LIVE AT THE WIRELESS

Darkside Lightside / Girl From Mars / Oh Yeah / T Rex / I'd Give You Anything / Kung Fu / What Deaner Was Talking About / Goldfinger / Petrol / A Clear Invitation To The Dance.

Death Star Records.

Produced by Philip McKellar.

February 1997.

Chart: 7.

SOURCES

ADDICTED TO NOISE
Live review, San Francisco by Clare Kleinedler, 7 August 1996.

BELFAST TELEGRAPH
Ulster's Rock by Ian McTear, 21 February 1997.

HOT PRESS
Digging The New Breed by Lorraine Freeney, January 1994.
'Petrol' review by Gerry McGovern, 24 August 1994.
Trailer review by Liam Fay, 30 November 1994.
A Festive Quickie With Mark Hamilton, December 1995.
Teenage Mutant Ninja Punks by Stuart Clark.
Ash! Bang! Wallop! by Stuart Clark, 24 July 1996.
Lydon Makes An Ash Of It, 24 July 1996.
Ash On Delivery by Olaf Tyaransen, 11 December 1996.

IRISH NEWS
Ash Won't Be Stubbed Out by Michael O'Toole, 3 July 1996.

JUST SEVENTEEN
Double Lazing by Piers, April 1996.

MELODY MAKER
'Petrol' review by Andy Cairns, 13 August 1994.
Cute Band Alert! by Ian Watson, 20 August 1994.
Live review, Belfast Limelight by Ian Watson, 27 August 1994.
Live review, Leeds Irish Centre by Lisa Hoftijzer, 5 November 1994.
Karate Kids III by Cathi Unsworth, 22 April 1995.
Mars Audiac Trio by Ian Watson, 5 August 1995.
Live review, Reading Festival, 2 September 1995.
Live review, London Astoria by Everett True, 3 February 1996.
Drugs'n'drugs by Ben Stud, 20 April 1996.
1977 review by Victoria Segal, 4 May 1996.
'Oh Yeah' review, 22 June 1996.
Live review, Belfast Mayfield Leisure Centre, 13 July 1996.
Embers Only by Everett True, 24 August 1996.
Merry Christmash by Tim Wheeler, 21 December 1996.
Live At The Wireless review by Ian Watson, 15 February 1997.

NEW MUSICAL EXPRESS

Live review, Islington Powerhaus by Angela Lewis, 14 May 1994.

Live review, Belfast Limelight by Simon Williams, 27 August 1994.

Trailer review by Emma Morgan, 5 November 1994.

Begorra's Banquet by Stuart Bailie, 26 November 1994.

'Kung Fu' review, 25 March 1995.

'Girl From Mars' review by Andy Richardson, 22 July 1995.

The Hash Street Kids by Simon Williams, 22 July 1995.

Live review, Bristol Fleece, 5 August 1995.

Live review, Manchester University by Mark Beaumont, 22 September 1995.

Hey Teacher! by Mark Sutherland, 30 September 1995.

Ash Fail To Bomb, 7 October 1995.

'Angel Interceptor' review, 7 October 1995.

Beamish & Butt-Heads by Stuart Bailie, 14 October 1995.

Live review London Astoria by Mark Sutherland, 28 October 1995.

'Oh Yeah' review, 20 June 1996.

Live At The Wireless review by Mark Beaumont, 15 February 1997.

TFI Friday by Steven Wells, 8 March 1997.

19

Ten Things You Should Know About Ash, 1996.

Q

No Ducking by Howard Johnson, June 1996.
Live review, Copenhagen Pumpehuset by Danny Eccleston,
April 1997.

RECORD COLLECTOR

Ash by Pat Gilbert, December 1995.

SELECT

Live review, Glastonbury by Gina Morris, August 1995.
Hangin' With The Homework Boys by Gina Morris,
August 1995.
Review of 1995 by Gina Morris, January 1996.
Stop That by Ian Harrison, August 1996.
Pacific Heights by Gina Morris, January 1997.
Its The Answer To The Universe by Ian Harrison, April
1997.

SMASH HITS

Ash Street Kids, July 1995.

SUNDAY LIFE

Families Blast by Stephen Gordon, 23 June 1996.
Ash Almost Split by Stephen Gordon, 30 June 1996.

SUNDAY WORLD

The Highs & Lows by Roisin Gorman, 23 February 1997.

THE TIMES

'Angel Interceptor' review by David Sinclair, 14 October 1995.

Interview by Leo Finlay, December 1994.

Turn Up Check In Rock Out by Steven Wells, December 1995.

'Angel Interceptor' review, December 1995.

Material World, July 1996.

THE FACE

NIGHT FEVER
CLUB WRITING IN **THE FACE**
1980 – 1996

When **The Face** was launched in 1980 it was the first ever monthly magazine to cover music, film, style and club culture.

From the early days of New Romanticism and New Wave to the Acid House boom and the huge change of culture that followed 1988's Summer of Love, **The Face** was there. From Hip Hop to Brit Pop it has explored new sounds, movements and lifestyles with unrivalled insight and integrity.

Night Fever brings together 17 years of club writing in **The Face** charting the development of club culture and the impression it has made on all our lives. *Night Fever* treads the cutting edge of music, fashion, dance and drugs from 1980 – 1996 to form an exciting and unique history of clubbing in the UK.

Published by **Boxtree**
25th July 1997
£9.99

MUSIC AND CULTURE
from BOXTREE

Please send me copies of:

❏	07522 2435 2	GETTING HIGH:	
		THE ADVENTURES OF OASIS	9.99
❏	07522 0227 8	PUNK: THE ILLUSTRATED HISTORY	
		OF A MUSIC REVOLUTION (HB)	16.99
❏	07522 2214 7	NIGHT FEVER: CLUB WRITING	
		IN THE FACE 1980 – 1996	9.99
❏	07522 2243 0	AEROSMITH - WHAT IT TAKES	9.99

TO: **Macmillan Distribution Ltd.**, Direct Customer Services,
Brunel Road, Houndmills, Basingstoke, Hants
RG21 6XZ, UK
TEL: 01256 302 699
FAX: 01256 364 733

HOW TO PAY

Please charge my Access/Visa/Amex/Diners Club for £ _____

Account Number _____

Expiry Date _____

I enclose a cheque for £ _____

payable to **Macmillan Distribution Ltd.**

Name _____

Address _____

_____

Postcode _____

Telephone _____ Signature _____

FREE POSTAGE AND PACKING!
UK and Eire only.
Please allow 28 days for delivery.
Prices and availability subject to change without notice.